To School Through The Fields

TO SCHOOL, THROUGH THE FIELDS

An Irish Country Childhood

ALICE TAYLOR

Brandon Book Publishers Ltd
Dingle, Co Kerry, Ireland

© Alice Taylor 1988

First printing May 1988
Second printing June 1988
Third printing July 1988
Fourth printing August 1988
Fifth printing October 1988
Sixth printing November 1988
Seventh printing November 1988
Eighth printing December 1988
Ninth printing March 1989
Tenth printing March 1990
Eleventh printing June 1990

Cover design: Paula Nolan
Typeset by Koinonia Ltd, Manchester
Printed in England by Clays, St Ives plc

To Phil, who was part of it all

Contents

Different Times

THIS IS THE story of a childhood. In its day it was an ordinary childhood but, with the changing winds of time, now it could never be.

Ours was a large family in a close-knit rural community that was an extension of our home. Neighbours came to our house and we went to theirs as freely as the birds flew across the sky; invitations were unheard of and welcomes unquestioned.

The old were never alone as the neighbours joined hands around them and the young, too, were included in the circle. As in every group of individuals, all had their own idiosyncracies, and we as children were educated in human awareness by the close association with many people.

Sharing was taken for granted, from the milk in the winter when some cows went dry, to the pork steak and puddings when the pig was killed. Work was also shared from the saving of the hay to the cutting of the corn and preparing for the Stations. It was an interlaced community and its structure helped those within it to support each other.

So please come back with me, to where we had time to be children and life moved at a different pace.

A Child's Nest

LISNASHEOGA WAS THE nest from which we learned to fly. An ivy-clad farmhouse surrounded by trees, it stood on the sunny side of a sloping hill at the foot of which the Darigle river curved its way through gold-furzed inches to disappear under a stone bridge into the woods beyond.

In the summers we swam in the river and caught minnows with jam pots; on Sunday evenings my father fished in it, bringing home each time a bag of trout. In winter salmon came up to this quiet backwater to spawn and, of course, there was a certain amount of poaching, to which my father objected strongly. Once, when a generous neighbour gave us a present of a poached salmon, he lined us all up around the kitchen table and proceeded to open up the fish. As the eggs poured out he explained about the huge loss of fish life due to the poaching of this one salmon. In my father's world nature possessed a balance and man had no right to upset that balance to satisfy his own greed; killing this fish was going against the laws of nature.

The river showed us two different faces of nature: in summer it was our friend but in winter it burst into brown torrents of anger that overflowed its banks and swept down our valley with a menacing roar. From the river valley the land rose and stretched away into rolling countryside, climbing into misty mountains at the

6

horizon. This was farming country, where the farmers and nature changed the face of the landscape with the seasons.

Our parents were a blend of opposites. My mother was kind and gentle, with a far-seeing wisdom, and she expected only the best from her fellow human beings. My father was a man with a high level of intelligence and a low threshold of tolerance; patience was not one of his virtues. He loved trees, birds and all his farm animals: nature he appreciated to the full, but he viewed his fellow human beings with a jaundiced eye and never expected too much from them.

With seven children in the family, we were reared as free as birds, growing up in a world of simplicity untouched by outside influences. Our farm was our world and nature as an educator gave free rein to our imaginations; unconsciously we absorbed the natural order of things and observed the facts of life unfolding daily before our eyes. We were free to be children and to grow up at our own pace in a quiet place close to the earth.

Preparing For The Stations

IN OUR TOWNLAND our turn for the Stations came around every six years and then it was like three Christmases rolled into one. The preparations might start as much as twelve months in advance as they provided an opportunity to get everything done in the house that needed to be done. The reason, of course, for this big clean-up was that Mass was going to be said in the house and all the neighbours for miles around were going to descend on us.

Broken walls in the yard were repaired and any gate pillar that had lost its balance suddenly found itself standing erect. Gates that had sagged previously now swung with free abandon. Loose sheets of galvanised were nailed down and missing slates replaced. Muddy grey walls became virgin white overnight and dunghills disappeared out of sight. The cows could be forgiven for thinking that they were in a strange farmyard and we almost expected them not to do what they always did.

The outside clean-up was insignificant compared to what went on inside: nothing from the roof down was safe. Mice and spiders that had nested comfortably for months suddenly found themselves in need of boating facilities as soapy water gushed around them. Broken panes of glass that had been patched up with bits of timber were replaced, sometimes a whole new window was installed. Bags of rubbish were burned indiscriminately and many a family treasure was reduced to ashes. Rooms that were full of clutter before, now doubled in size: we wandered around in a house full of hollow sounds.

When the burning and washing had finished the painting began and nothing escaped the paint brush. Ceilings, walls, tables and chairs all took on a new, bright look. It was the era of the slow drying paint and if you forgot to watch your step you could end up with a multi-coloured look yourself. The Stations only affected the downstairs rooms fully, but if a nosy visitor strayed off the main thoroughfare we were not going to be caught with our pants down.

Cleaning and painting finished, the next target was the big ware press in the parlour. Out came delicate china which had been in the family for years. My mother's respect for the Stations weighed against her fear of breakage, but the Stations won every time. Once when a precious jug was broken she mourned it for days, telling us all how long it had been in the family. Finally, Dan, our part-time travelling farm worker, said: "Missus, if it was here that long it was time to break it". And that was the end of that.

On the day before the Stations everything started to come together. The house was full of women polishing and setting tables. White linen table-cloths saw the light of day for the first time in years and moth balls rolled from between their creases. A strict eye was kept on the children, and for good reason. One year on the day before a neighbour's Stations all the good furniture was out in the yard while a new floor was being laid. The adults were busy in the house while the children, discovering a bucket of whitewash, proceeded to paint the dark mahogany furniture a brilliant white. Such potential catastrophes had to be borne in mind.

The night before the Stations had a special atmosphere filled with a sense of expectancy. The whole house lay in readiness, with fires set in all the downstairs rooms. Tables were laid with fine china and shining silver while bowls of lump sugar and dishes of butter rolls lay covered in the kitchen. In front of the fire was a row of polished shoes graduating from tiny tots upwards. We were all bathed in a big timber tub in front of the bedroom fire and we young ones were the last to be washed because our chances of getting dirty again were the greatest.

I doubt that my mother went to bed at all that night and if she did it was for a very short period. The cows got an early awakening in the morning and the milk was carried off to the creamery bright and early. Dirty jobs finished, everybody put on their finery. The large kitchen table was raised with a chair under each end to act as the altar. My mother was very particular about the altar, as for her this was what it was all about. She was a deeply religious person and the honour of having Mass said in her house was something which she appreciated to the full; on the morning of the Stations she had about her a special aura of peace. All the fuss of preparation was over and now, surrounded by her family and friends, because all her neighbours were her friends, she was going to welcome the Lord into her home. They were the two most important things in her life: her family and her God.

My father, dressed in his best black suit and shining soft boots – he never wore shoes – waited outside the door to welcome his neighbours and the priests when they came. It was grand to see the neighbours arriving, some having worked late with us the night before, but now all dressed up for the occasion.

Finally the priests arrived to a flurry of handshakes all around. One priest said Mass in the kitchen while the other heard confessions by the fire in the parlour;

it always tickled my fancy going to confession by our own parlour fire. There was a warm feeling about this Mass and communion, with all the neighbours gathered around the kitchen table. We had worked and played together and now we were sharing something much greater which formed a different bond between us. It was like the Last Supper.

After Mass the confession priest joined the other and dues were collected. A volunteer was sought for the next Station, which posed no problem as every house took its turn and everybody knew who was next. Then the flurry started: feeding the multitudes, but instead of loaves and fishes there was usually an abundance of goodies. Everybody helped so there was no panic, only organized confusion, and all were fed in the end. When breakfast was over the priests left and that was the official end of the Stations, but in reality it carried on all day and far into the night. Neighbours who could not come in the morning and maybe were not in our Station area came in the evening or even that night. Relations of varying degrees turned up and as ours was a long-tailed family this meant half the parish.

As well as a religious event it was also a social occasion. People came together who normally only worked together and visitors met old neighbours. Great talking was done. An impromptu concert often started up and anybody who could sing and indeed some who could not, entertained the light-hearted gathering. This evolved into a dance with a neighbour providing music on a melodeon. There was no shortage of energy and you would think that we had been resting up for a week beforehand.

After the Stations nothing could be found for weeks. Caps had disappeared and wellingtons were reported missing and many a man was left without his favourite old jacket. But who cared? We had had a great day and the house was fit to receive visitors from America for months afterwards.

Beneath God's Altar

O
LD NELL CARRIED her false teeth around in
her pocket. Our most eccentric neighbour, Nell
was often in trouble. Once my mother took her
to Cork to visit a doctor and afterwards they went into
the old Savoy for a meal. As soon as the waitress had
placed the meal on the table out came Nell's false teeth
and into the ashtray. My mother never batted an eyelid
and nobody would ever have known of this occurrence
but for the fact that my sister, who was working in Cork
at the time, had joined them, much to her regret. Why
Nell bothered with the teeth at all was difficult to understand: she did not use them for eating and you had only
to see her to know that, for her, appearance did not have
a high priority. The truth of the matter was that she
had paid good money for the teeth and regarded them
rather like the new hat which she wore for special
occasions. The fact that she ever acquired them in the
first place was entirely due to the considerable persua-
sive powers of the dentist, because making Nell part
with her money was like prising a stubborn barnacle
from a rock. She was not short of money. She was the
youngest of a large family who had all gone to America
and done well and, as they did not have marrying blood
in their veins, when they died Nell was the beneficiary.

She lived in a little house with a sagging thatched
roof where birds nested and swallows gathered every

year. The house itself was like a birds' nest and so over-grown with greenery that it was always dark inside. My father often tried to coax her to build a new house but to her that was out of the question, and she would not disturb the birds by repairing the old one. While things remained unchanged my father often said that he hoped the house would last longer than Nell herself and, indeed, it did.

Few of the neighbours called on her, not because they did not want to but because she did not want them to; she did not trust many people and preferred to keep to herself. Even when she called to our house she would start screeching about a field away: we heard her before we saw her. My father would raise his eyes to heaven and say, "Nell is beagling again". She had a high-pitched, quarrelsome voice and she shouted to you whether you were in the same room as her or a field away. When she came she was usually in a panic: the cows were after breaking out, or the donkey was stuck in a hole, or some other disaster had befallen her. And no matter what we were doing at the time we had to drop everything to go to her rescue. Nevertheless, she was not in the least bit grateful for anything that was done for her: as far as she was concerned virtue was its own reward. One day my father spent a few particularly tough hours trying to repair her thatched roof without disturbing her birds or falling through it himself. When he had finished she shouted out the door at him, "You are dressing a bed in heaven for yourself". The implica-tion was that he should be grateful to her for affording his soul such a golden opportunity.

If you met Nell without being prepared for the shock she would frighten the wits out of you. She had long black hair which she never washed and which was stiff with a combination of grease and soot. She had a straight black fringe, a little like Cleopatra's, except that Nell's was perfumed with smoke. A strange combination of dress and overall covered her from neck to ankles and down to her wrists. Her virgin skin never saw the light of day. She wore black knitted stockings and black leather boots laced above her ankles. Her face was almost as black as her hair and if she happened to have her teeth in they emphasised her overall blackness because from lack of use they were as pearly as the day the dentist gave them to her. When they were not in her mouth or her pocket they were soaking in a jam pot on the dresser, the only bright spot grinning in the semi-darkness of the kitchen.

I thought that Nell was a kindred spirit. Every day I called to her house and stayed there for hours. With that strange affinity which often develops between the very old and the very young we were in perfect accord. She did not comply with normal acceptable adult behaviour and in my eyes that brought her almost into my world, for to me she was more a child like me than an adult. We went to town in the donkey and cart and I was allowed to guide the donkey who had a mind of his own so we sometimes ended up in places far from where we had intended going.

With Nell I saw my first corpse. Some old woman who had gone to school with Nell had died many miles away, so we tackled up the donkey and set out. It was a lovely warm day and as the donkey stopped for a feed of grass whenever he got the notion it took half the day to go and the other half to come back. When we arrived at the wake house we were ushered into the room where the corpse was laid out; I had never before seen anybody dead and it scared the daylights out of me. Whatever she had been like in life, in death this old lady looked forbidding and aggressive. She was propped up in bed wearing a blue, high-necked frilled gown and her abundant hair was swept high on her head. Her face was grey and rigid. She looked as if she had spent her life giving out and that at any minute she might start again. I was glad when we made a hasty exit. Nell did not go in for social niceties and so, without exchanging any formalities with the other mourners, we boarded our donkey and cart for the return journey. I was half nervous that the old lady might be coming after us. I looked back. Everybody at the wake was out in the road looking in our direction. Nell had not bothered to say who she was and, as this was in a different parish, they had never seen her before. They probably thought she was the devil.

The only other regular caller to Nell's house was an old half- blind man called Tim Joe. He lived further back the valley and brought her any news that he thought she should hear; it was he who had brought her the news of the old lady's death.

Despite her lack of visitors, Nell decided that she would have the Stations when her turn came. She was not expected to have them but, contrary as she was, that was sufficient reason for Nell to do so. She sent word to all the neighbours via Tim Joe that she did not want them eating her out of house and home when they came, however. Undoubtedly they got the message, for there was none of her neighbours involved in Nell's Stations or the preparations apart from Tim Joe and me. And, compared with what went on in other houses, there were almost no preparations at all. My mother worried more about Nell's Stations than did Nell herself, but she was powerless to do anything as Nell, when she put her mind to it, was as unyielding as steel. The colour of Nell's altar cloths and the lack of anything for the priest to eat caused my mother sleepless nights, but they did not cost Nell a thought.

The day before the Stations Nell and I brushed the kitchen and threw out the ashes that sometimes accumulated if Nell did not get the urge to shift them. We whitewashed the inside walls and any parts of the outside not covered by ivy and, having washed out the floor and cleaned the windows, we thought the little place was a palace. Indeed, the cats and dogs that I had put out for the clean-up were nearly afraid to come back in. After our strenuous efforts Nell made tea and to my delight produced a currant cake, but while we were having our tea-party she saw through the window a curious neighbour approaching and straight away hid the cake behind a bucket of milk on the table. It was Nell's belief that it was more blessed to receive than to give.

After the tea, down from the smoky rafters she took a timber box. Before we had time to open it a brown mouse shot out between our fingers; his ancestors had probably moved in years previously and generations of his kin had been reared in the box. They were, of course, forced to live in such high places because of Nell's collection of cats which now gave chase and put a sudden end to the long, undisturbed tenancy. There was plenty of evidence of the mouse family in the box but apart from that and a few gigantic spiders the box was a store of treasures. It contained some lovely old lace cloths and brass candlesticks. We shook out the cloths and discovered that they had some gaping holes; these, however, did not bother Nell and she selected the two best ones to act as altar cloths. She had two hens hatching in boxes under the table but she decided not to disturb them; anyway, when it was covered by the white cloth the hens disappeared from view. And though the cloth was not perfectly white after long years in the box we thought that it was perfect, and we also used the candlesticks feeling no need to polish them.

On the morning of the Stations I arrived before the priests to find that Nell had no fire lighting: she refused to light it because the birds were not used to such an early fire and she would not upset them. Such reasoning could not be argued with: the priests would be there for only one morning, the birds were always there.

The parish priest was a kind, wise old man who, after evicting a few of Nell's cats from their warm bed, sat himself down on the chair beside where the fire should have been. The curate, Fr Kelly, knew Nell well and had a good working relationship with her: he agreed with everything she said. As he set up his altar I prayed that the hens would stay put and that he would not stand too close to the table as one of them was very cross and could stick out her neck and bite.

It was a peaceful sunny morning and the dogs lay asleep around the floor and the cats were curled up in the pool of sunlight on the doorstep. We had a heavenly choir as the birds chirped from their nests in the thatch and sang in the bushes and trees that grew wild and free close to the door. God smiled on us all that morning: it was a beautiful Mass and I saw a tear slip down the face of the old priest.

Suddenly, in the middle of the last blessing, the curate exclaimed, with extra vehemence, "Christ!" The old priest nodded kindly but I knew that the hatching hen had struck when I saw her head disappearing back through the folds of the altar cloth.

Mass over, the problem of breakfast reared its ugly head. In order to boil the kettle we had to light a fire, and lighting this fire was something of an ordeal. There was a hole under the open fire to create a draught and the bellows lay just beside to blow air into it. The problem was that ashes got into this hole and it had to be cleaned regularly, but Nell never cleaned it at all. Fr Kelly decided to tackle the problem. He lit bits of newspaper and pushed them in under Nell's black turf; they flickered feebly and, in order to encourage them, he went down on his hands and knees to blow at them. Unfortunately, Tim Joe chose that precise moment to turn the bellows, sending a shower of ashes over the head of the kneeling curate. Nell, who was chatting with the parish priest – or rather, shouting at him – then solved the whole problem in two seconds by pouring a jam pot of paraffin oil on the fire and set it roaring up the chimney. In no time the kettle was singing and Nell made tea as strong as porter. We boiled eggs in a black tin saucepan over the open fire, which was now glowing red and ideal for toasting bread. At last the five of us sat down and had a companionable breakfast, during which the hatching hens decided that it was time to stretch their legs and trotted out the door leaving evidence of their passage on the floor behind them. When Fr Kelly saw them a look of understanding came over his face and he smiled in amusement. Perhaps he had thought until then that forces other than divine were under Nell's altar.

When breakfast was over and we were relaxing in the sunny kitchen Nell retired to her usual chair by the fire and after a few minutes sent out a loud snore. The priests took the hint: their time was up. Nell was not accustomed to visitors and she had had enough for one day. I went to the gate with the two priests. The parish priest put his hand on my head and said, "Little girl, God is found in strange places. Try not to forget this morning". I never did.

Animal Nanny

IN THE FARMYARD the gift of new life came with the spring. After Christmas, when we had celebrated the birth of the child Jesus, the baby calves were the first to arrive in the animal kingdom. We had watched the cows heavy with calf trample daily through the winter mud; indeed, I had sometimes witnessed the commencement of this saga in the coming together of the bull and cow.

At night the cows were tied up in the warm stalls on beds of yellow straw and every night before going to sleep my father lit the storm lantern to go and see them. The lantern was filled with oil and had a lighted wick surrounded by a glass globe which protected it from the weather; this lamp hung from a long handle so that it could be carried comfortably by hand. In checking the cows nightly he had to be able to ascertain if any of them were going to calve during the night. He needed to be a bit of a gynaecologist as an unattended cow could get into difficulty calving and the result might be a dead calf in the morning. Many a night he went out in the cold of winter to check.

I loved to watch the baby calves arrive though I hated to hear the cows groan in pain; however, like all mothers, they recovered quickly once it was over. The new-born calf was put under the mother's head and she licked it dry. Soon it stood on its spindly legs and wobbled around before being picked up and carried to the calf house where it was put in a section by itself. The cow, after a feed of warm bran, would be milked and the beastings, as this milk was called, fed to the calf. At this stage he was not quite sure how to drink, so you put your fingers into his mouth and he sucked the milk off them. The cow never again saw her calf, which seemed cruel to me though it did not appear to bother her.

The calves were kept in their house during the cold weather where they were fed morning and evening with buckets of milk warm from the cows. It was one of the first signs of summer when the calves were left out and they were so accustomed to the limitations of house life that it took a lot of gentle persuasion to coax them into the bright sunlight. When we brought them through the haggard into a big green field they could not believe their eyes: they spread their legs and put out their noses expecting to meet a barrier; then took a couple of steps and tested with their noses again. They did this a few times until gradually it dawned on them that there were no more barriers: this was freedom. Then they took off, whipping their tails high into the air and galloping around the field with sheer abandon.

Each night they were brought back to the farmyard to be fed. They drank from a communal trough and had to be watched closely or they would drink too much as, like most teenagers, they still had to learn when to put the brakes on. One night I was supervising the feeding when one strong whiteheaded bull would not take his head from the trough despite all my efforts. Later on, while milking the cows, we heard a low bellow of pain coming from the haggard. My stubborn whitehead was prone on the ground with a swollen belly, his tongue hanging out and his eyes rolling in his head. Quick action was needed and my father pulled out his penknife and lanced the exact spot in the whitehead's belly. It receded like a balloon deflating and within minutes he was back on his legs. He had gone almost past the point of no return and I viewed his recovery as if he were Lazarus rising from the dead. My father took on a new dimension in my eyes.

As these calves grew older they did not need to return to the farmyard for feeding as they were able to eat sufficient grass for themselves. They were then kept in the fields, known as the inches, along by the river where they grew strong and during the winter cold when grass was scarce hay was carried down to them. However, if the snow came they had to be brought back up to the stalls for shelter. It was strange to see these calves, who but a few months previously had been nervous of open spaces, now terrified of the constraint of the stalls.

When spring came the large dunghills which had risen outside the cowhouses, stables and piggery during the winter were drawn by horse and butt to the fields, tilted out in heaps, and spread to make the grass grow. This was the only fertilizer used on the land and on the drills of potatoes, mangles, turnips and cabbage. The land which had been ploughed in winter or early spring was now harrowed and drills made ready for setting.

Setting the spuds was a big job. First my father sorted out the seed potatoes and cut them into *sciolláns,* a section with an "eye" from which the new growth would sprout. On the day of the setting we would each have a bucket of *sciolláns* – or a gallon if you were very small – and started setting at one end of the field. The drills stretched the whole length of a three- or four-acre field and if you looked too far ahead you could face that mental wall which long-distance runners meet. We had a cheery character called Mick working with us on the farm, and he shortened many a long drill with his stories. His advice in these or indeed many other circumstances was to "Keep your head down, your arse to the wind, and keep going".

If we were after having some wet weather the earth would be damp and clammy, clinging to boots, knees and hands. We went on our knees to set potatoes, wrapping jute bags tied with binder twine around them, and as the day wore on we were often weighed down with mud, which clung in lumps to boots and knees, and to add to the discomfort our hands got colder and colder while our noses were chilled enough to hang icicles.

If we all got fed up at the same time, which could happen coming on evening, we would all sit down and Mick would sing a song. We learned many songs while setting spuds and many a story was told, imaginary or otherwise. We understood well the story of the Gobán Saor, an old Irish legend.

The Gobán Saor ruled a large kingdom which he wanted to leave to the cleverest of his three sons. One day, he took his eldest son on a long journey and after some time walking said: "Son, shorten the road for me."

The son was totally at a loss as to how to help his father, so they returned home. The following day the Gobán Saor took his second son, and again the same thing happened. On the third day he took his youngest son and after they had travelled some distance he said once more: "Son, shorten the road for me".

The youngest son immediately began to tell his father a story that was long and interesting, and they became so engrossed in the tale that they never noticed the length of the journey. In our lives, Mick was the Gobán Saor's youngest son.

When all the spuds were set they were covered over with the dark brown earth and, even though we had suffered setting them, we felt a great sense of achievement the day the last drill was filled in. They stretched away into the distance, holding their secret growth within, and we knew every inch of that soft earth with the hidden stones that caused sharp pain when they came in contact with tender kneecaps. It would be difficult to be closer to the earth than we were.

We grew our own wheat, barley and oats. After ploughing and harrowing the land the corn drill was used to sow the grain. The drill was a long timber box with a hinged cover and into this the bag of seed was emptied. Underneath the box were long slender pipes that fed the seeds into the earth in regular rows as the horse drew the corn drill along.

When everything was planted it was in the hands of nature to provide the growth, and it was wonderful to see the earth returning our trust when the bright green growth burst forth. In spring the land wakes up from its winter rest, the grass emerges, the buds begin to appear on the trees and the whole countryside loses its threadbare coat. The birds start to sing again, telling us all that winter is over.

The spring also brought the young lambs. If there is anything that puts the "closed" sign on the door of winter it is the sight of frisky lambs playing in the fields. Sometimes, if the ewe decided that she was not designed for motherhood, a baby lamb would find its way into a box by the kitchen fire where it was bottle fed. Once I had such a pet and I called him Sam. He was cared for lovingly and by early summer he had grown to be a big fellow, able to follow me everywhere. One day, while I was stooped forward playing in the garden, he came from behind and butted me with his head. I was very offended by this ingratitude but it was evidence that Sam was ready to return to the flock; his pet days were over and he was letting me know in no uncertain terms.

On the poultry side of the farm the production cycle stretched across the summer months. In order to hatch chickens a hen had to get the hatching urge which motivated her to sit on a nest of eggs for three weeks. We had an old stone house at the end of the yard where rows of hatching hens sat in state in their boxes. They had to be fed and watered daily in the house because they all but refused to leave the nest. At the end of the three weeks the chickens chipped their way out of the shells and when they emerged they were soft and beautiful. The mother hen, or clucker as she was called, looked after her chicks with loving care and paraded around the farmyard leading her brood proudly. Sometimes, too, a hen might lay her eggs in a remote corner of the haggard and hatch them unknown to anybody; then one day she would march her chicks into the yard as if to say, "Look at me; aren't I clever?"

The turkeys, ducks and geese also hatched their eggs but took a week longer than the hens to do so. The goose liked to make her own nest and line it inside with soft down. The gander for his part was a most responsible father and guarded his goose on the nest; if you came too close he flapped his wings and stretched out his long neck to bite you. The young goslings were fluffy and yellow as butter and the goose and gander led them daily to the water where they all washed and swam around happily. But the males in the turkey and hen families were irresponsible fathers: once they had made their original contribution they disclaimed all responsibility for the consequences.

Great care had to be taken of the baby turkeys as they were a bit stupid and unlike the chickens and goslings had a tendency to get lost. The goose was a very good mother and she had a strong family unit working for her; the ordinary hen was the head of a one-parent family but her mothering instinct was fantastic. The turkey on the other hand had neither factor going for her: she was on her own and she was not unduly concerned about the well-being of her young. She needed a strong social welfare system to back her up and, of course, we provided that. Minding the turkeys was one of the chores of my young days. When they were set loose in a grassy field which was supposed to be good for them I was the social welfare officer who saw that none of them fell by the wayside. They had endless ways of going wrong. If they fell on their backs they could not right themselves; they could ramble off through the long grass and, with no sense of direction, get totally lost, and their mother would never bother to answer their plaintive "peep-peep". I liked this job because it was leisurely and did not require a great deal of concentration, so I could take a book along with me. Sitting on the warm grass on a sunny day reading was a pleasant way to while away the time, though occasionally I would forget what I was actually there for and would have to make a mad scramble to collect lost turkeys from all over the field.

A common enemy of all the young chicks was the hawk. He would circle around in the sky, observing, and then he would make a sudden dive, swooping down on the chicks, and soar off with one grasped in his taloned feet. He was accurate and deadly. The old hens were wise to his ways and if they saw him circling they cackled and set up a loud noise to alert us to the danger. We always came running to the rescue and clapped our hands at the hawk but sometimes it took my father's shot-gun to frighten him away. When I was very young I dreaded the hawk because I had visions of soaring skywards myself, caught in his fearsome talons.

The farmyard was a symphony of colour and sound. The hens were multi-coloured because they consisted of many breeds: there were Rhode Island Reds, the black Minorca with the golden beak, the white Leghorn and the frilly Sussex with her two white aprons giving her the appearance of a head nurse. Once they had produced their eggs they did not believe in hiding their light under a bushel, so they came out of the door of the hen-house emitting a high-pitched cackling noise telling everybody about their good deed for the day. The black turkeys gave off a continuous yodelling sound, the grey guinea fowl a single high- pitched clucking noise. We had the brown duck with their ringed necks and the soft-bosomed, voluptuous white ducks with their constant quack, quack. The geese seldom stayed around the yard as they preferred the open fields and waterways, but they came back at night to their own house; if they had stayed out the fox would have had a Christmas dinner every night.

There was seldom a fight between the different families on the farmyard as each one went its own way. If there was a fight it would be between the sow and the gander. The sow was not averse to thinking that a soft yellow gosling made a tasty mouthful, but before she could put her bad thoughts into action the gander, with outstretched flapping wings and with his sharp beak aimed at the sow's delicate snout and eyes, drove her squealing in the opposite direction.

Most of the new life on the farm arrived in the spring and early summer and almost all the births fitted into the ordinary farm proceedings. But the pig was not tied to any calendar month and her bonhams' arrival disrupted the normal routine. She was the one mother who required round-the-clock surveillance because she was quite capable of lying down on her baby bonhams and crushing them to death. This sounds as if the mother pig was a monster but how many mothers could cope with twenty babies at one go? It was enough to stretch even the strongest maternal instincts. The hen was the only other to come near her in number and she had just about a dozen. As well as that the hen hatched while sitting in comfort on her eggs for three weeks, while the poor old sow had the ordeal of labour pains and the messy job of physical production, and then finished up with twenty squealing bonhams which she was expected to breast-feed. It was a tough job and it was no wonder if sometimes she felt like sitting on them.

When the bonhams were due the sow started to make a bed wherever she happened to be. She was put into a little house by herself with plenty of straw or hay and proceeded to chop up the straw with her mouth and tease it out with her crubeens. She kept working on the bed until she had everything settled and her nesting instinct satisfied. Finally she settled down and got on with the real business of the day. The litter of pretty, pink bonhams could vary from twelve to twenty in number and if there were more than the sow could cater for they had to be bottle fed. When it was feeding time the sow grunted with a loud, regular rhythm and all her little ones got the message straight away. Between feeds they lay cuddled up together against the mother. The need for supervision came when the sow got up and had to be let out for a walk or just wanted to stretch her legs, for when she returned to lie down she never checked to see where her bonhams were. She just flopped down and if they were in the wrong place she lay on them and killed them. In fairness to the sow, with the best intentions in the world it was impossible to keep her big brood out from under her legs. This was where we came in, using a brush to get the bonhams out of the way quickly.

The bonhams learned fast and after a few days they could look out for themselves, but while they were very small somebody had to stay up at night to mind them. The first time I was ever allowed up with an older sister to mind the bonhams was of a Friday night as we had no school on Saturday. I was delighted because I was curious to know what a night up was like. At that time we had a big open fireplace in the kitchen and we banked it up with turf for the night. The sow only required checking at regular intervals so, apart from that, our time was our own. We played cards and made an apple tart. At about two o'clock I sat on the old sofa by the blazing fire and must have dozed off because the next time I heard the clock strike it was four in the morning.

It was midsummer and the dawn was breaking when I went out into the garden. It was bathed in a pink translucent light and a soft mist lay along the river valley. I was mesmerized by the absolute beauty of the morning and the dawn chorus in full volume from the trees around the house. It was one of those rare moments of perfection that are imprinted in the memory forever.

A Touch Of Spring

Spring came today
And walked with me
Up the hill
Breathing softness in the air
Opening gates within my head
The birds felt his presence
Pouring forth symphonies
Of unrestrained welcome
It was mid-January
And he just came
To have a peep
Trailing behind him
Along the valley
Wisps of purple veils.

Forever Young

AS CHILDREN WE all loved Bill. Though of our father's generation he had not closed the gate of childhood behind him, and we knew this instinctively. He did not talk down to us but met us at eye level. He lived on the top of the hill beside our home; part of the hill was an ancient fort and at the foot of it was a fairy well. At that time farmers' houses lacked piped water so all drinking water was drawn by bucket from the local well, and every night without fail Bill brought a bucket to our house. So regular was this bucket that when calculating our fresh water requirements we automatically counted in Bill's contribution.

When he arrived after supper his first task was to teach us our lessons. His patience was endless. Maths, catechism and Irish were all done diligently but English was his favourite; he read profusely and his reading took precedence over all other activities in his life. I remember one sunny day coming on him sitting on a grassy bank reading Shakespeare when every other farmer in the neighbourhood was busy saving hay.

My father often despaired of Bill's farming methods and was constantly urging him to be more efficient. At that time artificial insemination had not come to the bovine world and some farmers kept a bull to provide the necessary service; Bill availed of our facilities for his cows. One summer morning my father met him coming across one of our fields trailing a rope behind him; he was, he told my father, bringing a cow to our bull. When my father enquired as to the whereabouts of the cow Bill turned to discover that there was nothing at the end of his rope! His thoughts, no doubt, had been on less mundane matters.

Bill had a stone cowhouse with a thatched roof mellowed to a soft creamy white by years of sun and rain, while the cows had fashioned their own windows by gently butting their heads through the thatch. Milking time presented a pleasant picture with each cow's head protruding through the low roof, contentedly chewing the cud and looking out over the farmyard. The yard was always spotlessly clean, though some of it through lack of use was covered with soft green moss and the timber gates were weather-beaten to an almost grey-white smoothness that had a silken texture beneath your hand. An old grey donkey completed this peaceful scene.

As a child this was my retreat corner. Being the youngest of a large, noisy household this hilltop haven often provided a welcome escape when older sisters proved too much to handle. Here there was nobody to boss or annoy me or to make me move any faster than I wanted to; Bill and his two old sisters had all the time in the world and were delighted to see me.

His two sisters were the bane of his life. They ran the house with clockwork efficiency and expected him to run the farm in the same manner. But though they were of the same family Bill was cast in a different mould to his sisters. He never believed in doing today what he could put off until tomorrow, and they pursued him relentlessly in order to make sure that nothing was put off. He devised many ploys to outmanoeuvre them so that he could enjoy his reading in comfort. At the far end of the haggard was Bill's rick of hay and into this, on the side facing away from the house, he cut a large hole with the hay knife, and the fact that it faced the sun was an added bonus. In his sunny seat Bill sat, totally oblivious to the world around him and safe from the pursuing sisters. This plan worked for a long time until one day the dog and the gander had a fight and chased each other around the rick of hay. Eventually, the gander got a reeling in his head and collapsed. One of the sisters, who had watched the fight, came running to investigate the condition of the gander. Bill had also watched the fight and, thinking it hilariously funny, roared with laughter, which his sister on hearing traced to his retreat corner, where all his books told their own story. That was the end of that hideout.

Bill lived close to nature and if the summer was very warm he swam nude in our river, in a pool that was clean and fresh and full of brown trout. This gentle giant of a man – he was a splendid figure standing over six feet – would dive from the cliff into the pool and swim like a giant fish. I found his knees very impressive: male knees were rarely seen in rural Ireland at the time, shorts being an unknown mode of apparel. Other, more intimate details of his form did not provide the same interest as specimens of male reproductive organs were part of the animal survival pattern of everyday life on the farm.

During the long summer holidays the plague of lessons did not exist, so Bill joined in our many games. One of our pretend games was shop, which we played under the trees in the grove. We nailed rough planks between the trees to display our goods – empty cartons collected from the kitchen and from neighbours – which we arranged along the shelves, and we erected a makeshift counter in front. Here we traded for hours using pebbles collected from a nearby stream as currency, and though the rate of exchange posed no prob-

lem, the price of each item was open to long and complicated negotiations. It was up to the shopkeeper to sell
the goods, with a convincing argument as to their value,
and it was up to the customer to buy as cheaply as possible. Bill always joined the row of customers when he
came after supper, and he brought new and colourful
arguments to bear on the shopkeeper. Everybody
wanted to be the shopkeeper as we felt that this was
the leading role, but Bill turned the tide in favour of
the shopper.

During the winter holidays card playing and dancing
replaced the lessons, and we were often joined by other
neighbours who came visiting. Playing cards was the
only occasion on which Bill could lose his temper: if
anybody cheated he put his head down like an angry
bull, threw his cards on the table and tore out the door.
Being completely honest himself, he would not tolerate
the slightest deviation from the straight and narrow
path of right. The dancing, however, posed no problems.
We all lined out around the kitchen while somebody
wound up the old gramophone, and then we hopped off
the stone floor, ranging in age from seven to seventy.
The fairy reel, set dances and barn dances were executed
with more gusto than skill until everybody was
exhausted and collapsed into the *súgán* chairs that had
been pushed back against the walls. My mother then
put the kettle on over the open fire and when we had
recovered our breath and cooled down we all gathered
around the fire for cups of cocoa.

Bill and my father had gone to school together and
were friends all their lives. There existed between them
perfect understanding, though they were very different
types of people. To Bill my mother was a welcome extension to his own life and he loved all of us unquestioningly; indeed, in some ways we were a three-parent
family, and Bill was a plus in our lives which we took

for granted. When he died quite suddenly it came as a hard, sharp blow. He died at home and the wake took the usual form of the time with all the neighbours rallying round to give help and support, but for some reason I did not go anywhere near the house. On the day of the removal I went to the highest field in our farm, overlooking Bill's home, and from here I watched the hearse leave the house, and tried to come to terms with the concept of a world without Bill.

After the funeral one of the sisters came and asked my mother if one of us children would go and stay with them for a while. It was Easter holiday time, so we were all at home. There was no great rush on the invitation but to me the idea of trying to ease their loss of Bill was strangely appealing so, putting my night-dress under my arm, I set out happily back through the field behind the house. Coming to the fairy well I lay on the large mossy stone in front of it and gazed into its dark green depths. Then I ran up the steep hill, stopping to sit on all Bill's resting places which he had made during his lifetime.

I do not remember how long I spent with the sisters but it was a whole new experience. Here life was lived at a defined pace. The amount of water to go into the kettle was measured, the number of slices of bread needed for the tea was calculated. Nothing was left to chance, everything was ordered and regulated. One of the sisters was in a wheelchair and from there she ran the house down to the very last detail. To me it was fascinating because it was such a complete contrast to our house.

Not everything had changed, though. I would walk around the grey stone yard, into the white-thatched cowhouse, and rub my hand along the silken timber of the weather-beaten gates. Here was a timeless existence. Below the house was a long narrow garden

shadowed by overhanging trees and filled with daf-
fodils. I lay among the green and yellow rows and gazed
up into the sky through the soft green leaves. I saw Bill
smiling down between the clouds, which was no great
surprise as heaven was just above them and Bill was
sure to be there.

The Long-Tailed Family

W E CHILDREN WERE very attached to the farm animals. Some of them were older than ourselves and very much part of our home life; not alone were some of our animals born and reared on the farm but so also were some of their mothers and grandmothers, and a lot of them died of old age and were buried there. Our burial ground was at the bottom of the orchard and here the jennet, when he decided that he had had enough and lay down and died, was laid to rest. All our pals, including cats and dogs, got an official burial and at times we marked the graves with little timber crosses.

The horses held a special status on our farm. We had a red bay called Paddy and a grey mare named Jerry and the jennet who, because he was the only one of his species on the farm – or indeed in the parish – was just called the jennet. He was a strange animal, smaller than a horse, bigger than a pony, and with the face of a donkey. I once heard John Dillon say on radio that the jennet "did not have pride of ancestry or hope of succession; he was, in other words, a non starter". It was a harsh pronouncement, giving the jennet nothing to look back at and even less to look forward to. However, it did not seem to bother our particular fellow: black and long-tailed, he brayed like a donkey and kicked like a devil and if you stood too close to him he

37

might decide to sink his long yellow teeth into you to see if you tasted good. One of his jobs, which he did every day, was to go to the creamery; he could find his own way to town and stopped along the route at houses where my father regularly gave in gallons of milk. He was a real loner and he did not fraternise with the horses or the pony. However, he had one thing in his favour: in the morning, when my father went to the gate of the field and whistled, he came willingly, not needing to be called a second time or coaxed on his way.

Catching the horses, on the other hand, was a job that had to be done most mornings and sometimes they were very uncooperative. Some people are reluctant to get out of bed early to face a day's work, and likewise horses are loath to be rounded up to face their day's labour. My eldest sister, Frances, was the one who loved the horses most and she usually went out to catch them early in the morning; if she got close enough she would swing off Paddy's mane and jump on his back for a gallop. One morning she had on a pair of loose wooden clogs that were a fashionable necessity during the war, but when she had Paddy galloping the clogs fell off under his belly and frightened him. He bolted. He raced up the fields like a streak of red lightning, but the effort of coming up the steep incline to the yard slowed him. He arrived in the farmyard frothing from the mouth and covered in sweat, Frances clinging to him like a leech. She had enjoyed the challenge of holding on, while I watched with my heart in my mouth.

Of all the animals that belonged on the farm, it was Paddy's death that caused most trauma in our house. He was older than I and was a horse with great class. In animals you get as much individual variation as in humans: there are the mean, sly, stupid, intelligent and honest ones just the same as us. Paddy was the cream of the animal world. He would neither kick nor bite and was hard-working. He was also an honest animal – if you think there is no such thing as a dishonest animal then you have never heard of a thieving cow. Some cows always have their heads up to see if there is something better in the next field and if there is, up and over they go to get it. We have that much in common with the cows. With horses, when they worked in pairs there was the one who pulled hardest and did the most work; there was also the horse who had no mean traits and was loved and respected by his owner. Such a horse was Paddy.

At the top of our farm was a wild area known as the Glen. It was bushy and rocky and the horses seldom went there. One spring morning, however, when my father went out to bring them in from the fields Paddy was not with the others. After a long search he was found lying in a deep hollow in the Glen. My father's heart must have stood still when he saw him: Paddy made an effort to rise but was not able. When the news got back to the house we were shattered and all made a bee-line for the Glen. There he lay, unable to rise, whimpering in distress because he could not follow us home. That day in school, instead of the blackboard I saw Paddy lying in that hollow. I was completely distracted for lesson after lesson and got many slaps, but it felt as if they were hitting someone else. The clock dragged slowly around to three.

When I got home I learned that the vet had come during the day and had pronounced that Paddy had broken his back and would have to be put down. It was like a death in the family. We all knew that my father would do the needful; a shot would be quick and merciful, but it would be so terrible for my father who had worked with Paddy for years and loved him dearly.

I went by myself to say goodbye. Going up to the Glen in the dusk on that late spring evening was a sorrowful journey. There was a soft mist falling and I felt that even the leaves were crying. I climbed down over the rocks to where Paddy lay in the grassy hollow; he whimpered when he heard me coming and turned his dark, moist eyes in my direction. Sitting beside him I stroked his silken face with its white star. He nuzzled me gently and, as I put my arms around him, my tears ran down his neck. He neighed softly and looking up I saw my father silhouetted against the darkening sky. He had his shotgun with him. It was time to go.

Walking home through the soft wet grass I waited to hear the shot break the silence of the evening. When it did not come I knew that my father was waiting for me to get home first. I sat on a stone to wait and at last it came like an explosion in the quietness of the Glen. After a while my father came down the rocky path. There was no need to say anything when he saw me. I put my hand into his pocket and we walked home together.

Close To The Earth

Come to a quiet place,
A place so quiet
That you can hear
The grass grow.
Lie on the soft grass,
Run your fingers
Through the softness
Of its petals,
And listen:
Listen to the earth.
The warm earth,
The life pulse
Of us all.
Rest your body
Against its warmth;
Feel its greatness,
The pulse and throb,
The foundation
Of the world.
Look up into the sky,
The all-embracing sky,
The canopy of heaven.
How small
We really are:
Specks in the greatness
But still a part of it all.
We grow from the earth
And find
Our own place.

Celebration Of
The Seasons

EACH YEAR WE welcomed summer by erecting a
May altar in honour of Our Lady. In this we were
motivated less by religious fervour than by a
wish to celebrate the long, warm days by bringing the
outdoors into the house in bunches of wild flowers which
we picked along the ditches and in the open fields. In
the bedroom over the kitchen was a large old chest with
deep drawers. Over this we draped a white sheet and
on top of it we put a box slightly smaller than the chest
top and covered this with another cloth. Then another
box, slightly smaller again, with another cloth, and so
on as high as we could go without causing the whole
thing to topple over. On top of this pyramid we perched
Our Lady. This was her altar, so she got pride of place,
but she was not to have it all to herself. On the steps
below her came statues of Our Lord, in case he might
feel overlooked, and then Blessed Martin and St
Theresa. Also included was St Philomena, but she was
actually there under false pretences as the Vatican in
later years changed their minds about her credentials.
Then came the flowers and greenery arranged in jam
pots and trailing down from step to step.

When we were finished we regarded our creation as
a masterpiece of sanctity and in front of it we knelt and
prayed, feeling that at any moment we might sprout
angelic wings and soar heavenwards. Such was our

sense of drama that we draped ourselves in trailing bedspreads with pillow covers as haloes on our heads and danced in front of the altar.

One day Connie and I decided that we would bury ourselves in the drawers of the old chest. Maybe we had visions of the popes buried beneath the Vatican. Connie got into the bottom drawer without mishap but as I attempted to settle into my proposed tomb the entire creation of devotion tilted forward and collapsed on top of us. The crash was thunderous, with statues, jam pots, flowers and water flying in all directions. Everybody downstairs in the kitchen came running up the stairs to investigate. We scrambled out of the drawers and under a large old timber bed in the corner of the room where nobody could get at us since the bed almost touched the floor and they were all too big to get under it. My mother was annoyed when she found that Our Lady had lost her head; our sisters were raging over the complete mess, and my father gave out because it took very little to start him off and he thought that we were a holy terror anyway. We stayed under the bed for a long time until things calmed down but we finally ventured downstairs when Bill came as he could always be relied upon to pour oil on troubled waters. Our Lady later acquired a concrete neck which was a bit thick, so she lost some of her swan-like elegance but it was the best repair that could be achieved at the time as fixatives had not yet come on the market.

As soon as the sun had taken the cold sting out of the weather we wanted to cast aside our heavy winter clothes and don our summer dresses but my mother put her foot down with her old adage, "Ne'er cast a clout till May is out". In winter we wore heavy tweed skirts with hand-knitted jumpers and beneath them grey flannel petticoats. Under the petticoat came a sleeveless jacket called a bodice and then a pure wool long-sleeved vest.

We wore long black woollen stockings up as far as possible and secured in place with garters and long-legged
knickers with elasticated ends to just above our knees.
We spent cold days out in the fields and sat in a damp,
draughty, unheated school, so the need to be warmly
clad was imperative. But when the weather grew warm
we were glad of the freedom that bare limbs afforded.

My mother made all our clothes and for summer wear
she bought us a large roll of cotton material and ran up
simple, shift-like slip-over-the-head dresses. The prim-
ary need was to cover our nudity and elegant cut was
not a requirement. Climbing trees and slushing
through muddy gaps was not conducive to model child
appearance, so clothes were serviceable rather than
flattering.

Each of us girls had a box in which we stored our
summer dresses in a big press over the winter. Come
summer we brought our boxes out into the garden to
lay them out to air in the warm sun. In our garden all
the plants and shrubs were called after the people who
gave them to my mother, and escalonia was Jer Lucy's
bush. On that day Jer Lucy wore a collection of gaily
coloured dresses. As the youngest of five girls I was
reared on a succession of hand-me-downs but I had a
godmother in America who sent me parcels of beautiful
frilly muslin and silk dresses which smelt of lavender
and foreign places.

When the sun had warmed the heart of the earth it
thrust forth white garlands of little button mushrooms.
They came up overnight in small clusters where late
the night before there had been nothing but green. Now
there they were, with their little white faces peeping
up from between blades of grass. Some fields were mushroom fields and others were not, and we knew where to
look, but so did all the neighbouring children. Where
mushrooms were concerned it was a free-for-all with

farm boundaries of no consequence. So, if mushrooms were on your mind you rose early because as well as other early pickers there was the fact that cows and horses could trample them into the ground.

Gathering mushrooms in the early summer morning, with the dew washing your toes and the thrill of discovery growing with each white cluster, was a lovely experience. Sometimes, stretching like gossamer across the grass, the dew-glistening cobwebs sheltered the little mushrooms, almost like a mantle protecting them from the world above the earth. Finally, gallon full, we skipped home through the sun-warmed fields to savour our collection. We cooked them for breakfast on red hot sods of turf beside the fire. Each white mushroom was placed on its back, in its pale pink cup a shake of salt which melted and mingled with the juices as it cooked. Picking it up, careful not to spill, first you drank it and then you ate it, a little chalice with the liquid and flavour of the open fields. Sometimes my mother boiled them in milk but somehow that was to reduce to the ordinary this food of the earth that needed no preparation as it was bathed in the morning dew and could be eaten as picked, such was its delicacy and freshness.

As the summer progressed the briars along the ditches burst into blossom with green berries that later matured into large, luscious blackberries which arched and draped themselves around every field, ripe for the picking. Each blackberry was inspected on picking to see that the stem base was free from small tell-tale holes, the tracks of tiny snails that feasted on the blackberries, especially when the rain brought them forth in great numbers; any blackberries with these signs were returned to mother earth. First we ate what we could contain, developing purple-smudged mouths and fingers; then we filled gallons and buckets to the brim. My mother made large two pound pots of blackberry jam, most of which were consumed at a rapid rate, but some of which were stored to bring the taste of summer to the winter months.

Crab apple trees grew in some of the fields but the crabs were small and bitter; however, they could be made into a sweet- tasting jelly and jam. Picking them was a thorny business as often strong briars and blackthorn branches were entwined in them. Once, having filled a bucket of crabs, I left it in the middle of the field while I drifted away to follow some other diversion. Coming back a few hours afterwards I found that my bucket and its contents had been baptised in amber liquid: of all the places in this wide open field for the cow to stand to do the needful!

My father often came home with his cap full of crabs and once he asked me how valuable I thought a cap full of crabs was; when I answered, "No value really", he smiled and said, "Well, a child who does not respect his fellow human beings is as valuable to the human race as a cap full of crabs". He did not expect much from his fellow human beings but he was very conscious of the rights of other people and always instilled this consciousness in us.

We had a very happy young lad called Christy working with us. He loved dancing and was often out until the small hours of the morning as he also had an eye for a pretty face. One night, coming out of a dance in the local hall, he found his bike punctured so he helped himself to a tube of another one as he had a girlfriend to take home on the bar of his bike. Incredibly, Christy was later taken to court and sentenced to six months in jail for this offence. My father was stone mad about it, feeling that Christy was a gay-hearted lad and that the punishment was outrageous in relation to the crime. When Christy came out he was quiet and subdued and all his old sparkle had gone. On his first Sunday back my father and mother went away for the day, leaving all of us children and the house and farmyard in Christy's care. A few days later he went to visit his mother.

"Christy," she asked him, "will they trust you on the farm after being in prison?"

She afterwards told me that he smiled as he said, "It made no difference: they went away on Sunday and left me in complete charge." She said that it did more to restore his self-esteem than any amount of words could have done. And, indeed, Christy soon regained his self-confidence and was his old sunny self again; my father had never studied psychology but he had an innate understanding of human nature.

Wild fuchsia, which we called bell trees, grew along the hedges and, plucking off the bell-like flowers, we sucked their sweet, sticky juices as we had seen the honey-bees do. If thirst overcame us out in the fields fresh spring water ran along by most ditches, flowing down from the hill behind the house. We were expert at leaning into greenery and, using our saucered hands as cups, we scooped up the crystal-clear water and drank from the palms of our hands. The only polluters of the waterways were the ducks and geese and my father often objected to them as the horses and cows often refused to drink the water after them. My mother, however, stood up for their rights and refused to listen to his objections, stating that as they used only one large stream they were entitled to their freedom and the pleasure they got from the water.

As summer turned to autumn we stored the best apples for Hallowe'en, or Snap Apple Night as we called it. We diligently watched the nut trees, hoping that they would be ripe in time, but ripe or not we always picked them. These trees were tall with high, arching branches far from the ground, so it took all our climbing skills to conquer them. We climbed to the top and then as far out along the swaying branches as we dared, while we swung up and down at precarious angles, grasping bunches of nuts and throwing them down to the collector on the ground. Finally, gallons full, we slithered to the ground and danced home through the gathering dusk, scratched but triumphant. That night we cracked our nuts with a stone on the flagstone before the fire while apples swung from cords tied to the meat hooks on the rafters of the kitchen or floated in the timber tub of water in the middle of the floor.

For Christmas too the land provided what was needed, and the Sunday before we made our annual pilgrimage to the wood for the red-berried holly. It was there in abundance as was the ivy and moss, together with strange, interesting pieces of dried-out timber. We gathered them all and tied them up in bundles with hay twine and we brought them home on our backs, holding firmly to the twine across our shoulders. They would all be used to make different decorations for Christmas. There was no money for shop decorations but we did not need them as all around us the countryside fulfilled our needs.

The Jelly Jug

SUNDAY IN THE country was a day of complete rest. Cows were milked, animals and humans fed but, apart from that, we all took time to ourselves. It was a holiday in the kitchen as well so that everyone would be free of the work routine. Unfortunately, we had to rise earlier than usual so that the cows were milked before the early Mass to which my brother went on his way home from the creamery. This left my father free to take the rest of us to the late Mass.

My father was always present for the breakfast on Sunday, and it was a very relaxed occasion as there was no work waiting to be done. It was the only time he ever sang and his favourite was "The Old Bog Road". He would tilt back his chair and, rubbing the back of his head with the palm of his hand, he would rumble "her coffin down the old bog road". He had a voice like a rusty chain rattling in a bucket but what he lacked in harmony he made up for in enjoyment because he only sang when he was happy. He liked poetry and was much better at reciting that than he was at singing. His favourite poet was Goldsmith and *The Deserted Village* rolled off his tongue with such relish that you knew he approved of all the poet's sentiments. He also had an odd little poem which I never heard from anyone else:
Once upon a time
When pigs were swine

And turkeys chewed tobacco
And little birds built their nests
In old men's beards.

Once the Sunday morning poetry session was over he turned on the Church of England service on the BBC saying, "Listen to them now; every bit as good as what we will be hearing from our own in an hour's time".

The pony's job was to take us to Sunday Mass in the trap. This could be a hazardous undertaking in the winter because if the pony slipped on the ice we would all end up out on the road on top of our heads, but in the summer it was a very pleasant way to travel. If we passed anybody walking along the road they were picked up and brought to town. At that time the different premises in the town had backyards where the horses and traps were tied up during Mass. After the ceremony we would call to an aunt's house with a bastable cake from my mother and two large whiskey bottles full of milk and our aunt would offer us tea and apple tart.

Then my mother did her shopping. This was of a very practical nature as money was scarce in those days: there was plenty of everything except money but then the need for money was not great. We produced all our own food and most places we went to we walked, which cost nothing only time, and we had plenty of that. We children stretched our pennies to buy those sweets which cost the least and lasted the longest. The best value was a sixpenny slab of toffee, for which my sister Phil and I pooled our resources, and that lasted us a whole week. It was the lap of luxury to have something to chew on going to school and sometimes it did a two-way journey as we took it out of our mouths half chewed and saved it, wrapped in paper, for the way home.

Sunday in the country was a leisurely day. As well as shopping after Mass, much chatting was done when my mother met her neighbours and often the talking took longer than the shopping. My father went to the pub for a few pints and met up with his friends. We went to change our books in the branch library which had opened in our town, and although it took much browsing and deliberating it opened up new horizons for us. Finally we all drifted back to the pony and trap, with my mother always the last to arrive and my father now nicely relaxed as he lit up his pipe and puffed away contentedly. When we were finally ready to go home the pony trotted off at an easy pace.

Arriving home we had what we called a tea dinner – nobody worked on a Sunday so there was no cooking done, and we usually had a cold meat salad with jelly and cream afterwards. My mother often made jelly the night before for this Sunday treat: I loved making jelly too, and watching it melting under the hot water always fascinated me. One day I put my jelly into an orange jug, not realizing that it was a family heirloom which my mother had got from my grandmother when she married. I poured the boiling water straight from the kettle on to the jelly and the jug split in two halves. I can still see the red jelly flooding out over the table as my mother's gasp of horror conveyed the enormity of my crime. Years afterwards, when I was the same age as my mother was when this happened, we were discussing the orange jug.

"Do you know something," my mother said, "I think that the pieces of that jug are behind in the old turf house in a hole between two stones under the back window."

And back I went into the semi-darkness of the old stone house that was now used for storage and there, exactly where she had said, between the stones under the window, were the pieces of the old jug. It took me back years just to see it. I was delighted and brought it

51

away with me to have it repaired, and it now takes pride of place in my collection of jugs. My mother was a hoarder, a trait that proved a great blessing for us too in later years.

After the dinner on Sundays my father usually went fishing, a solitary pastime from which we were excluded for fear of frightening the fish. But we enjoyed catching the flies that he used. He put a piece of fresh horse dung into a box and this drew the flies; then he closed the box, which had a round opening at the other end, and up against this he put a cow's horn. The flies flew into the horn which he then covered with mesh wire, and the horn full of buzzing flies slipped nicely into his fishing bag. When he came home the bag was usually bulging with brown trout. We washed the fish in the stream at the bottom of the garden and my mother fried them in butter for the supper.

We children usually spent Sunday in the fields. Sometimes we just lay quietly in the long grass watching the rabbits, of which there were dozens along every headland, and if you appeared suddenly they would scamper into the ditches and down their burrows. The ditches were riddled with burrows: very occasionally you came on an extra-large one and this was the fox's lair which was also easy to recognize on account of the strong pungent odour that hung around it. Sometimes, too, you might see the fox running at an easy pace along by a bushy ditch and stopping every now and then with ears cocked for danger. Once ever I saw one out in the open: he ran the entire length of our long fort field where I happened to be sitting at the top of the rise. When he saw me he stood still and stared at me. If he was frightened I was even more so because I had visions of being carried off between his jaws like my mother's hens. We stared at each other for a few seconds and then he sauntered off, dismissing me as of little danger.

Picking wild flowers was another Sunday pastime: the buttercup, the bluebell, the woodbine with its haunting smell, all found their way back to our kitchen where they stood in every corner in empty jam pots. As well as acting as a flower vase the jam pot served many purposes: it kept the goose grease from the Christmas killings, which was used for softening tough shoe leather and easing painful joints; it also served as a fishing net for catching collies, miniature fish that travelled in shoals. We tied a twine around the jam pot's neck and laid it on the river bed where it sparkled between the stones. Standing motionless beside it we watched the collies swim around our toes, tickling them, until one invariably found its way into our pot and then we swung it out of the water. We often caught other types of fish as well but we were scared stiff of eels, convinced that they would bite the toes off us.

Some Sundays we went to the fort which was just behind our house, a very big fort where my father had planted trees years before, so now it was a wood as well. Set on the side of a sloping hill it had huge mounds with hollows in between, and the entire place was carpeted in pine needles so that walking felt like treading on cushioned air. We played hide-and-seek around the mounds and behind the trees and the only sounds beside ours were the birds'. The place was a haven for all kinds of wildlife and here too the foxes often made their head-quarters – much to my mother's annoyance because her geese and turkeys often became their prey.

We had a series of birds' nests which we visited, care-ful never to disturb anything as we watched the eggs increasing in the nest. We were delighted to see the baby *gearrcaigh* (or nestlings) appear and often hid our-selves to watch the parents fly back and forth feeding their young. Every year the swallows came to our cow stalls and stables where the rafters were a maze of nests,

and it was a great feather in your cap to be the one to see the first swallow and to hear the first call of the cuckoo. At night we fell asleep to the sound of the corncrake whom we thought said:
"Corncrake
Out late
Ate mate
Friday morning."
At that time meat was never eaten on Friday so the corncrake was breaking the fast.

In the grove below the house the pigeons cooed continuously. In the orchard beside this grove my teenage brother started beekeeping, but as his hives increased he moved to the grove behind the house. Here a hive was stationed under every tree and it was absorbing to watch the bees at work, especially in the summer when my brother sometimes went away for a week on a beekeeping course and I was left in charge. The first time this happened I prayed that they would not swarm, but of course they did. One afternoon when I came to check them, there, hanging off a branch like a large cluster of grapes, was a fine thick swarm of bees. I knew the procedure and though a trifle nervous I donned the beekeeping gear. Approaching quietly, with one hand I held a bucket just below the swarm and with the other I hit the branch a good belt with the back of a hatchet and the swarm fell neatly into the bucket. A share of the bees buzzed angrily at this intrusion into their peace but I put the bucket under the tree and when they had settled covered it with a sheet. Now at least they could not take off if the notion took them, which was quite possible anytime before sundown.

Late in the evening I returned to finish my job. Having found the old door of light timber which my brother kept for this purpose, I rested one end of it on the landing board in front of the hive and the other end on the ground, and then covered it with a white sheet. Gently lifting up the bucket I prised the covering off and shook the lump of bees out onto my prepared sheet. At first they buzzed angrily but soon they got their bearings. The trick at this point was to spot the queen, who is a good deal larger than the other bees, and make sure that she went into the hive so that the others would follow. I had beginner's luck: there she was heading for the front door, so the rest followed on naturally. There was no need to stay after that as they did the rest themselves, but I came back later in the semi-darkness to check that the sheet was clear of bees. The grove was peaceful at that time of night with all the hives silent after their busy day. If you knelt down beside a hive and put your ear against it you could hear the soft drone within. Our kitchen table was never without a honey supply, whether it was a jar, a section or indeed sometimes a frame of honey straight from the hive.

My mother was the only one of the family to spend her Sunday in the house. She sat inside the open kitchen window reading the Sunday papers, and she always had interesting articles from the weekday papers put aside to be read on her day of rest.

At this time, as well, she had the radio to herself. This was a great luxury in our house as there was usually a power struggle when different channels had interesting programmes on at the same time. My mother was an avid radio listener all her life. At that time *Mrs Dale's Diary* was on BBC at 4.15 every weekday and she never missed it; indeed, we often ran home from school ourselves to be in time to hear Mrs Dale if she was having a family crisis. *Woman's Hour* was another of my mother's favourite programmes.

However, her peaceful Sunday reading and radio listening was usually interrupted as she had many callers; this, especially, was the time when neighbouring farmers' wives came to visit. Apart from these my mother had a varied assortment of visitors. There was one lady gone past her first flush of girlhood, but not realizing it, who came to my mother to get her a husband or a "little job". My mother baulked at the first suggestion but set her up in many "little jobs". Invariably though, things did not work out and back she would come again looking for another little job. She smoked like a trooper and when we came into the kitchen and sniffed her cigarettes we annoyed my mother intensely by saying: "Oh, you had 'little job' today".

Another Sunday evening caller was Andy Connie. He was an uncle of my father so he must have been fairly old, but he had the heart and fitness of a teenager. Leading in to our outside yard was a five-foot-high gate, and into the garden a smaller one, and he never opened either one but jumped over them. He loved singing and dancing and often stood in the middle of the kitchen floor and danced a jig or a reel. He just danced because he was full of the joy of life and we loved to see him coming as he was like a ray of sunshine.

Andy's wife had died at a young age and he was left with a baby daughter, whom he adored. Many of his friends tried to get him to remarry so he composed a little poem to put them off. Mary Barry had been his wife's maiden name and he invoked her support in his dilemma:

If Mary Barry of old
Could only behold
Her own Andy Connie
Getting married again.
Her corpse long dead
In her narrow bed
In anger and shame
Would rise again.

Andy stayed with us one stormy night and the following morning at breakfast he told my mother that he hadn't been able to sleep at all as the ash tree at the bottom of the garden was all night calling, "Andy Connie, Andy Connie". To this day the tree is known as Andy Connie.

Towards evening, when we all drifted back to the house, the Sunday night jobs had to be tackled as the animals needed to be fed irrespective of what day they had. Two of us went to bring home the cows and two more to feed the calves and someone to feed the hens and other fowl. After milking we all had supper together and there was usually some extra treat because it was Sunday. Then my father went roving and the older ones went dancing but my brother usually had to hive his swarm before he went anywhere. My mother usually went for a walk in the fields, coming back then to finish her reading. Later, when my father returned, she rounded up the members of her household too young or too old for night life and we all knelt to say the rosary.

An Odd Old Codger

OLD GEORGE WAS different from the other neighbours. He lived by the letter of the law and if you came into close conflict with him he could run you up the steps of a High Court before you knew how it happened. As far as I know he never studied law but he knew exactly how far he could go without illegally infringing on anybody's rights. He was meticulous in his ways. He drove into town in a pony and trap, the pony fat and well groomed while you could see yourself in the gloss of the shining trap. He wore a dark suit and a black bowler hat and spoke in a slow, measured voice that gave one the impression that he checked every word before it passed his lips. He was not greatly liked but he was part of the place and we accepted him for what he was, an odd old codger. Everybody kept well away from him: rather like our jennet, he was safer at a distance.

A new Guard came to town and decided to flex his muscles with George. We could have told him that he was on a loser but bright young men, then as now, know it all. He called on George to check on his dog licence. At that time the Guards kept a close watch on the canine population and if you were caught without a licence you were summonsed and taken to court. This young Guard asked George if he had the dog licensed and George said no, he hadn't. The Guard cautioned George that he would be back in a week and wanted to see the licence then. A week later he was back and George gave him the same answer.

In due course a summons arrived and George went to court. He loved going to court: maybe at heart he was an actor who loved a dramatic performance. The case was called and George was summoned to the witness box; the judge, remembering this client from previous experiences, decided to play it cool.

"You appear to have an unlicensed dog," he said mildly.

"I have not," George answered.

"But that is the charge," the judge said.

"The charge is incorrect," George announced.

"But you do own a dog?" the judge queried in an effort to get things straight.

"I do not own a dog."

"Well who owns the dog in question then?" the judge asked.

"My son Peter," George answered, "owns that dog."

"And why is he not licensed?" the judge demanded.

"That dog is licensed. My son Peter has got him licensed. I do not own him so I do not license him!"

George enjoyed challenging the establishment. The priests at that time carried mighty clout, or so they thought. Every house in every townland had the Stations in their turn and it was the custom that the house due to have the Stations collected the priest's suitcase from the house in the adjoining townland which had had the Stations the previous day. The suitcase contained the priest's requirements for saying Mass and though this system probably originated when the priests travelled around on horseback it still continued with the arrival of the motor car. It suited the priest and nobody thought to question it: that was, until George came up against it.

On the morning of George's Stations everything was in readiness when the priests arrived. As was customary the parish priest went into another room to hear confessions while the curate, who was a self-opinionated, middle-aged man, started to get his altar ready. He looked around questioningly for the suitcase which was usually in readiness. It was nowhere to be seen. "Where is my suitcase?" he demanded.

Quite unperturbed, George replied, "I suppose, Father, it's wherever you left it. That's nobody's business but your own."

From then on the priests carried their suitcases themselves.

When George died after reaching a fine old age all the neighbours flocked to the house for the wake. His wife had died years before and his son Peter was a pleasant man who had often found his father's approach to life a little perplexing. Wakes could often be sad occasions but George's was almost a celebration: he was different in life so it was fitting that he should be likewise in death. After a night of storytelling and drinking, the neighbours decided to say the rosary in case it might look as if they had forgotten what brought them; Jim, who had worked with George for many years, decided to take charge. George's sense of drama must have rubbed off on him because in order to give out the rosary he decided that he required an exalted position. He climbed up on the kitchen table where he knelt over all the others. "The man at the helm steers the ship," he declared, and then proceeded to say the rosary in a loud, measured voice exactly like old George.

Holiday Hens

HOW DO YOU live to a ripe old age and still believe that this is a wonderful world and everybody in it as good as they can be? My mother never lost her faith in the goodness of human nature. If anybody wronged her she invariably excused them, reasoning that they would not have done it if there was any alternative open to them. Her simple logic often caused frustration. We had one neighbour who enjoyed a good gossip, and the juicier it was the better for telling: he believed that you should never spoil a good story for the sake of the truth. If he was really scratching the bottom of the barrel for a listener he fell back on my mother, and he always lived to regret it. No matter how startling his news, she was totally indifferent, remarking: "Never heard a word about it", with the implication in her voice that if it had been true she would have heard it.

"Blast it, Lena," he'd say, "it could be on the tay bag and you wouldn't hear it."

One day in desperation he dismissed her totally from his potential audience, telling her in a withering voice: "You are no company because you won't say a bad word about anyone".

Despite this implicit belief in her fellow human beings she could still cut you down to size, but so gently that it might be ten minutes before the implications of

61

what she had said would hit you. One of my sisters and I once had a long and complicated argument with her and finally were convinced that we had proved our point and totally outmanoeuvered her. She smiled innocently at us and said: "For a stupid woman, how did I have two such clever daughters?"

My mother included all old neighbours as part of our household duties and because she was so tolerant she was often imposed on. One of her friends sent us her hens on holiday every year while she and her husband went to the seaside. Not alone did the hens come on holiday but they had to be collected by my father in the pony and crib, and this put him into a rage that lasted for the entire length of the hens' visit. But if my father objected to the whole idea, it was nothing compared to the hens' objection for hens are settled creatures and do not like strange places. Neither do hens make good hosts, and our own hens made the visitors' lives a misery and fought with them in every corner. In fact the only one delighted with the situation was our cock. This extended harem brought new life to his flagging spirits but by the end of the month even he had had enough of this particular pursuit and was in a state of exhaustion from over-indulgence.

Bedtime posed the biggest problem because, whatever about the cock, hens are very selective about whom they let into their beds. So, come dark, the residents retired to their hen-house while the visitors took to the trees. This might have been an ideal situation but for the wily fox, for when dawn came the foolish hens would come down off the trees and then he would strike. A loud squawking would wake the entire farmyard and out of bed we would all tumble, my father swearing vengeance on the hens and the fox and waving his gun. Total chaos reigned in the soft light of the new day. The horses objected to close gunfire at dawn and the complete bedlam woke all the other animals. Pigs who had been sound asleep and cuddled up together comfortably suddenly awoke with the clamour and decided that it must be much later than they thought and that they should be hungry. Hungry pigs set off a high-pitched repetitive peal which penetrates the toughest ear-drums and tightens the most relaxed nerves. All hell broke loose and the culprits were, of course, the visiting hens.

The only solution was to get them into bed voluntarily or otherwise every night. This could not be achieved until they had settled for the night. The spot of their choice was usually the tops of the trees in the surround-ing grove. The older and more submissive hens we had rounded up and driven into the hen-house at dusk. But a lively pullet determined to get away is not easy to pin down, so on the tree tops we had the lively young ones who had to be grounded and housed.

When dark came and they were all settled we issued forth from the warm kitchen armed with brush handles and long sticks to poke the reluctant hens from the branches. We younger ones enjoyed the climb to the tree tops in the dark. Having grasped an unfortunate hen we sent her flapping to the ground where she was bundled up by an adult and thrust into the hen-house. This operation could take up to an hour, during which time my father cursed and swore at the hens, but not alone at them but also their owners – "Daft bastards tanning their arses in Ballybunion".

All this extra night-time activity took place in August at the peak of the haymaking and contributed greatly to frayed tempers on hot days in the meadow. If Dan was with us at this particular time he would announce at breakfast to all and sundry and looking at no one in particular, that "People usually get what they deserve". Dan had great respect for my mother and got on with her as well as his cantankerous nature allowed, but her easy-going ways sometimes drove him to distraction and he certainly blamed her for "these blasted hens" that were upsetting the whole home.   After a month everybody had had more than they could take, so when the owners returned bronzed and rested my irate father packed their holiday hens into the crib, tackled the pony to it and brought home their charges. I often wondered how he resisted telling them what to do with their hens. But even though her calm acceptance of other people's problems drove him to the outer regions of a nervous breakdown, he loved my mother greatly and would do nothing to hurt her family or friends. "Don't upset the wife's people," was one of his favourite bits of advice.

Open Spaces

PAUL'S FARM STOOD on the hill across the river from our house. He had spent many years out in the Australian bush and was accustomed to the solitary life, having no desire for human companionship. His male neighbours he tolerated but women seemed to be outside the realms of his comprehension and he kept as far as possible away from them, viewing them as members of a dangerous species that threatened his safety.

His neighbours respected his privacy and kept their distance, and if he needed help at any time he would stand on the hill outside his house and shout across the river. If trained in operatic circles his remarkable vocal cords might have brought him fortune, their volume and vocal range were so extraordinary. A neighbour almost as well endowed was Jack, who lived to the west of us, and it was not unusual for a long-range conversation to take place across the valley, and we used to listen happily to the shouted communications of what we called the Lisnasheoga telephone.

Paul had long white hair with a matching beard and wore a loose white, flannel waistcoat to his knees. In summer he peeled off his pants and went around in his white long johns. He presented a strange biblical appearance out in his meadow on a summer day. Once ever he was unfortunate enough to be taken ill and had to go into hospital. It was the small local cottage hospital where a domineering matron ruled with a rod of iron: that is, until she met Paul. For a man who had spent most of his life out under the stars a rigid hospital bed was a new and unwelcome experience. The matron insisted, however, that the bedclothes be tucked in firmly, but as soon as her nurses had achieved this Paul whipped them out again. A battle of wits and words raged daily between Paul and this iron lady who confirmed all his worst fears about women. Finally, one day the matron herself tucked in the bedclothes so rigidly that Paul was almost strapped to the bed. In a glorious fit of pure rage he gave such a violent tug at the bedclothes that he turned the whole bed upside down. From underneath the bed pouree a tirade of abusive language describing the matron in terms hitherto unheard. Paul won the battle and his bedclothes hung freely from then on: a free republican bed of defiance in a ward where absolute dictatorship was otherwise the rule of the day.

Paul attended no Sunday services. His God was out in the fields with him and as he did not think too much of his fellow human beings he could not see how they could be of any assistance in getting him into heaven. Our saintly old parish priest accepted Paul's thinking but he moved to another parish and a new priest arrived who believed that conformity was the road to salvation. He rode a saddle horse and one day called on Paul. Without even showing him the courtesy of dismounting, this priest lectured him from his superior position in the saddle. Paul listened wordlessly, but when the priest hesitated in order to gauge the impact of his words Paul raised the stout crop that he always carried and brought it down sharply on the horse's rump. The startled horse bolted out the gate and was halfway back to town before the priest succeeded in bringing him to a halt. He had discovered that Paul might send him to heaven a lot faster than he could get Paul there.

Paul lived to a ripe old age and despite his innate distrust of women it was one of that dreaded species, in the person of a kind cousin, who cared for him lovingly at the end of his days. One hopes that heaven has open spaces for someone like Paul, who never liked to be fenced in, or maybe his spirit is free to ramble along by the banks of the Darigle river where he herded his cattle and saved his hay.

Back To Simplicity

Oh, clergyman all dressed in black,
What a mighty church is at your back.
We are taught that by your hand
We must be led to our promised land.
Jesus is locked in your institutions
Of ancient laws and resolutions,
Buried so deep and out of sight
That sometimes we cannot see the light,
Behind huge walls that cost so much
Where simple things are out of touch.
But could it be He is not within
These walls so thick, with love so thin?
Does He walk on distant hills
Where long ago He cured all ills?
Is He gone out to open places
To simple people, all creeds, all races.
Is Jesus gone from off the altar
Catching fish down by the water?
Is He with the birds and trees,
Gathering honey from the bees?
Could it be in this simple way
That God meant man to kneel and pray?

Mrs Casey

MRS CASEY LIVED two fields away from our house. She had never heard of Women's Liberation but she was herself a liberated woman. She was an integral part of our lives and attended our coming and going as she laid out the dead with dignity and love, and welcomed new-born babies with open arms. Babies at that time had the luxury of being born at home where they were welcomed not alone by parents but by grandparents, aunts, uncles and caring neighbours.

Eight generations of our family have lived in our house and Mrs Casey was present to welcome the first of the seventh generation when my parents' first-born arrived. Waiting with my father on the night in question were my maternal grandmother and my uncles, but when the nurse finally brought the new-born son into the kitchen it was Mrs Casey who, with her great feeling for place and tradition, stretched out her arms and said, "Welcome to Lisnasheoga, James Nicholas!" This was no wrist-tag baby whose name was as yet open to question: this was a child whose grandfather's name was waiting for him and whose roots in this very house stretched back through many years.

After that first son my parents had five daughters, which Mrs Casey regarded as rather unfortunate; baby girls she accepted but did not rejoice in. Then, on a cold

January night, my younger brother Connie was born. Mrs Casey had a healthy respect for the spirits of the dead and the "little people" as she called them, so, when my father called to her on his way into town for the nurse and the doctor, she lit a blessed candle and holding it high above her head she walked from her cottage to my mother's bedside with the candle still lighting. "They came with me when I had the blessed candle," she told my mother.

She had a strong, implicit faith. Once, she was very ill just before Christmas, and the doctor told her to stay in bed; however, on Christmas morning, as she afterwards told my mother, "I felt that I'd get up and go to Mass, so we tackled the black pony. When I went into the church I went to the holy water and washed my face and hands in it and the strength flowed back into me."

She was her own faith healer. She held nothing in awe, only the spirits of the dead and the "little people". She was convinced that the "little people" of the fort helped our family. But it was not within the power of man or animal to frighten her. Most women find rats a frightening sight but when one made an unwelcome intrusion into her bedroom she bundled him into a towel and choked him.

She regarded being childless as one of the worst afflictions that could befall a couple, and when this was the case with a neighbouring couple she ascribed it to the fact that when the husband went to bed he went to sleep. As a little girl I remember her making this pronouncement to my father, who was highly amused, while I was intrigued and felt that it had implications beyond my grasp. She was very tolerant of the weakness of human nature and if the first baby arrived ahead of schedule to a newly married couple she always smiled kindly and said:

"Wasn't it great to have so much done before they got

married".

She loved children and could see no wrong in them. If any one of us was in a sulk and my mother was trying to straighten us out, Mrs Casey would say, "Don't cross them". That was her full philosophy where small children were concerned and we still quote it. Mrs Casey was a great believer in the natural order of things and breast-fed all her children whenever and wherever the necessity arose.

She had great faith in marriage as a builder of character. If any selfish young woman who always had to have her own way was getting married, Mrs Casey would smile wisely and say, "The baba will straighten her out."

Or if the head of the family was very troublesome and aggressive, she would remark, sagely, "His own will level him; it always takes your own to level you. The same bad blood is in the veins, you know."

The dead she attended with loving reverence and a thoughtfulness all her own. When Mike, an old neighbour, died suddenly Mrs Casey did the needful. This old friend had always worn a hat and when he was laid in the coffin Mrs Casey told my mother, "He looked so cold and not himself without his hat on. So I looked around and there was none of his own to be seen, but on the sideboard beside me was a small black hat. I put it on him and pulled it down over his ears and he did look better and more like himself, so we closed the coffin on Mike with the hat on."

As the hearse was moving out of the yard his sister came looking for her hat. Mrs Casey recalled afterwards: "I knew then that he'd be back. He had the hat and he'd come back for her." Strangely, the sister died within the week.

Mrs Casey worked hard all her life both indoors and outdoors and knew few luxuries. Every year she fattened two pigs in a Baby Ford car parked in the garden of her cottage. They announced their hunger pangs by putting their heads out of the windows and squealing to be fed. When they were the right weight she had them killed and salted and put into two timber barrels at the bottom of the kitchen. She loved her food and could eat large amounts of fat meat but never suffer indigestion. Early in their married life her husband made the mistake of praising his mother's cooking. As she told my father, "I took it from him for a while, but then one day I stood back and gave him a swipe of the *ciotóg*."

She was left handed, and always referred to her left hand as "the *ciotóg*", almost as if it belonged to someone else. Any problem which she failed to settle amicably brought the *ciotóg* into action.

Her husband was a dapper little man with a neat black moustache and she always referred to him as "My Jack", or "My little man". He loved his porter but was drunk after two pints. At a time when women seldom frequented pubs, Mrs Casey always stood at the counter with the men to have her pint. Similarly, at the Stations the men usually had breakfast with the priests while the women ate elsewhere, but Mrs Casey never failed to seat herself at the priests' table and often brought them to task about any matter in the parish which she felt was not in order.

Every year she planted fourteen drills of potatoes in one of our fields and she dug them out with a spade, while Jack followed on, picking them into a bucket. It was a very long field, with a rise at the top, and sometimes she would be gone over the rise and out of Jack's sight. If my father came on them, she would look back and say, "He's failing, my little man is failing".

Then, further back, Jack would say to my father: "I have to let her forge ahead, you know. She'd think that she was failing if she couldn't keep ahead of me."

They had each other's measure and were very happy together.

Mrs Casey picked potatoes, cut turf, thinned turnips and bound the corn. Cutting the corn took place in early autumn when my father, with two horses tackled to the mowing machine, usually started the work on a mellow September day. One of us children, sitting on one seat, guided the horse while my father, on a lower seat, would create the swarths suitable for the sheaves. All around the field the workers would bind up the corn into sheaves. Mrs Casey worked across the bottom of the field and always had the way cleared before the horses. The cutting started at the outside, working all around the field and gradually, as the day wore on, the swaying corn turned into golden sheaves which were then stood in stooks before night fell. Mrs Casey worked hard all day, her small sturdy figure dressed in flowing black moving back and forth. Sometimes her hearty laugh pealed across the field as she enjoyed a good-humoured exchange with a neighbour. She understood her neighbours and if she did not like them she never pretended otherwise, but with those she loved her great heart knew no boundaries and she brought colour and richness into their lives. She had a wealth of character and though the winds of change blew around her they never carried her with them. She was a strong woman and her philosophy of life was all her own.

Earth Woman

She was as real
As the dark brown
Bank of tiered turf
With the promise
Of warmer days.
She was as solid
As a great oak,
Unbending with
The winds that blow.
She was as strong
As the hard rocks
That weather the
Crushing waves.
Her core had
The luxuriant glow
Of the black, rich,
Sensuous soil.

Tea In The Meadow

WHEN THE SUMMER had proved its intention of staying with us, cutting the hay began. With his meadows ripened to a honey coloured hue by the sun, my father went to the haggard and, taking his old mowing machine firmly by its long shaft, he eased it slowly from under the overhanging trees where it had sheltered throughout the long winter.

A simple, solid machine with two small wheels and drawn by a pair of horses, it had a raised seat for the driver at the back. On one side was a cutting knife which lay flat on the ground when in use and was raised up for the journey back and forth from the meadow. Inside this knife was a long blade with diamond-shaped edges called sections. At first my father oiled and greased the entire machine, which had seized up during the winter; then he sat astride the shaft of the mower and laid the long blade across his knee. There was a skill in edging the blades in which he took a particular pride. He had a long edging stone with a timber handle, which he kept on top of a high press in the kitchen. This was taken down and inspected and when found to be in perfect condition was the cause of great satisfaction. What could possibly have gone wrong with it is difficult to imagine, but I suppose he had discovered over the years that very few of his tools were safe from his energetic brood. Now, sitting in the warm, sheltered haggard, beginning at one end of the blade and taking it section by section, he edged along with a balanced rhythm, occasionally dipping his stone in a rusty gallon of water which stood on the ground beside him. Gradually the rusty, archaic blade assumed a new life, its teeth gleaming with a razor sharpness, and along its base lay a ridge of brown and grey froth like the moustache of a monster man. I sometimes sat on the ground and watched this deadly weapon come to life, in awe of its power for my father gave us strict instructions regarding the dangers of farm machinery and the use of his gun, and his commands were obeyed unquestioningly.

The following day cutting the hay did not commence until the sun was high in the sky and the gently swaying hay was well dry of the morning dew. Paddy and James were rounded up, eager for work as they were after a long rest since the spring ploughing. That had been heavy, cold work and they had come home at night with their hooves covered in mud, but the hayfield promised to be soft and pleasant underfoot, with ample juicy mouthfulls available to satisfy any pangs of hunger.

The two horses were tackled to the mowing machine and, arriving in the meadow, they cut the first swarth along by the ditches and continued all day around the field, their rounds becoming gradually shorter. My father always watched out for birds' nests hidden in the hay, and the one most likely to be found was the pheasant family. If the birds rose from the hay he would halt the horses and walking into the high grass he would gently lift up the nest and carry it to the mossy ditch. Some nests, however, did not transport very well and once he brought home a few pheasant eggs to be put under a hatching hen. They hatched out along with her chickens but they were much smaller and far more active. When they grew bigger they were carried to the fort where several families of pheasants lived, and there they returned to their own lifestyle.

The blade of the mowing machine gave off a plaintive whine which carried across the valley and told of busy times. And so, hour after hour, my father and his horses worked in companionable silence while all around them lay the moist swarths of newly mown hay. Coming into the meadow in the late afternoon, bearing a jug of tea and home-made brown bread, I was enfolded in a wild, sweet essence that was moist and sensuous, stimulating some deep-rooted feelings in my inner being.

Now my father sat in a shady corner under a tree and drank his tea straight from the jug, while the horses also relaxed and sampled some freshly cut hay, flicking their long tails to keep the flies at bay. I explored the newly exposed ditches around by the headland, as we called the outer edge of the field after the first swarth was cut. In some of the meadows a stream ran along by the ditch and here floated all kinds of interesting insects sheltering under the overgrown grass and ferns. Here too, earlier in the year, frogs' croak was to be found, a jelly-like substance encasing an abundance of black dots trailing little floating legs, the baby frogs in neo-natal condition. Those tiny tadpoles who had squirmed out of that quivering quagmire were now grown into frogs of all shapes and colours: there were yellow, green and sometimes black frogs to be found jumping along the moist ditches of the meadows.

The rabbit families lived on the other side of the meadow where conditions were drier. The whine of the mowing machine and all the unexpected activity in their quiet corner had sent them scurrying under-ground, but now, while there was a temporary lull, they ventured out to see what was going on. They stood trans-fixed in amazement to find their familiar scene totally changed; gone was the high sheltering grass, and now the entire meadow lay exposed before them. But then, seeing the horses and humans, they turned tail and disappeared, to return no doubt when all was finally quiet and their domain was no longer disturbed by human intruders.

One of the meadows had a complete hedge of wild honeysuckle or woodbine, as we knew it, and this sent out a soft, wild, heady perfume that mingled with the smell of new mown hay. You had to stand still and close your eyes to fully absorb this feast of fragrances.

When my father resumed cutting I usually stayed on, wandering around, exploring mossy ditches and picking wild flowers, until finally the last swarth fell and the day's work was over. The long knife raised, the horses felt the sudden easing of their straining chains and set off briskly towards the gap that led to home. Here was a stream of spring water where they drank, spattering spray with their quivering nostrils. Back in the haggard they were relieved of the burden of the mowing machine and tackling; then they trotted off to the freedom of the green fields with only the dark patches where they had sweated beneath their tackling to show that they had spent a hot day working in the meadow. Often times they lay down on the cool grass and rolled over on their backs, with legs cycling in the air. Then, righting themselves, they jumped up and galloped around the field, exulting in their freedom from restraining ropes and chains.

The next step in the cycle of haymaking depended on the weather and if it was less than perfect a process known as turning the hay had to be endured. This was sometimes done by hand with a hay pike: the swarth of hay which was now dry on the top side had to be turned over and its damp underside exposed to the sun. It was a slow, monotonous process which could raise blisters on little hands unaccustomed to gripping pike handles for long, but the monotony was relieved by the companionship of many people working together. Often-times this job was done by a machine, aptly named the swarth turner, and why it could not always be used I found hard to understand, but maybe on some occasions manpower was more plentiful than horsepower. The swarth turner was a strange looking machine on two extremely large iron wheels with two timber shafts to the front, and to the rear two giant iron spiders that sped around tossing the hay in all directions, exposing it to the sun and air. It was drawn by one horse and the driver sat on an iron seat perched high over the twirling spiders.

When the hay was sufficiently dry it was raked into rows with the wheel raker, a machine similar in design to the swarth turner which pulled a giant iron rake behind it. This gathered up the hay and then the driver pulled a lever which raised the rake, leaving the hay in a tidy row; down banged the rake again and the next row was collected. The aim was to have each row of hay parallel to the previous one and this required split-second timing and good horse control. That was the ideal, and when it was not achieved the driver of the wheel raker would be subjected to much derogatory comment from his or her fellow workers.

And so at last we arrived at the actual point of haymaking. The interval between cutting and hay-making could vary from two days to two weeks, depend-ing on the weather, but the shorter the interval the better the hay. Hay, fast-dried in the hot sun, with all traces of green and moisture evaporated, was far superior to a dark brown version that had soaked up rain and had to be shaken out to be re-dried. Haymaking and wet weather made bad working companions and turned a pleasant experience into a long-drawn-out hardship. However, when the sun shone all these dif-ficulties were quickly forgotten. When the swarths were ready for saving the meadow was full of blond, crinkling hay. The smell of the hay had changed, becoming more aromatic and varied as it matured, and on the day of the cutting the meadow was perfumed with a wild, sweet fragrance that filled your nostrils with the essence of summer.

A day in the meadow was sunshine and sweat, hard work and happiness. Hayseeds and innumerable forms of insect life found their way into your hair and clung to your damp back. We were usually barefoot so we picked up numerous thorns, but this annoyance was relieved by the soft feel of mossy patches beneath our feet and we developed a second sense about where it was safe to tread. Luckily, some of our meadows lay by the river, and oh! the joy on a hot day to plunge into the icy water and rid yourself of all this sticky irritation.

A contraption called a tumbling paddy was used to collect the rows of hay into big heaps. Made entirely of timber it was like a giant comb with two handles at the back; when it was full to overflowing with hay the handle was thrown forward so that the comb tumbled over and all the hay fell out. This was then used as the base for the cocks of hay, or wyndes as we called them. When the butt had been made somebody stood on it and packed the hay down while the tumbling paddy collected more hay which was piked on to the wynde until gradually it grew tall and pointed.

Standing on the wyndes was a job for somebody light and agile. Pikes of hay were thrown up at you and had to be pulled in under your feet and danced on to firm this wavering creation. Sometimes the hay would hide an odd scratching briar or a soft yellow frog to stimulate an unplanned high jump. Things going to plan, however, you slid down the side of the wynde when it had reached its peak, then it was pared of loose hay at the base and finally tied down. A piece of hay with its ends firmly embedded in the base of the wynde was wound around the hay twine and knotted with it. The ball of twine was then thrown across the wynde and tied at the other side in the same way, and this process was repeated crossways.

And so it continued all day, wynde after wynde, while we got hotter and thirstier as the heat beat down on us. Then somebody would call in a voice full of elation: "The tea is coming!"

My mother usually brought the tea in a white enamel bucket and maybe a tin sweet-gallon full as well. We made ourselves comfortable on various heaps of hay and passed around cups of tea with slices of homemade brown bread. We watched my mother's basket eagerly and usually she came up trumps with a big juicy apple cake. It is said that hunger is a good sauce but hunger and thirst certainly made the tea in the meadow a feast with a special flavour, like manna in the desert. The aroma of the sweet-smelling hay blended with the tea, funny stories and riddles made for great laughter and fun, and the whole occasion took on the atmosphere of a gay picnic.

Tea over we got back to work but there was new pep in our step and gradually the wyndes rose like mini pyramids around us. Towards evening, as the shadows lengthened across the field, we gathered up our rakes and pikes, and together with the horses made our weary way homewards. Sometimes, though, one of the more energetic members of the family would shout: "Race you home!" and we would all take off, weariness forgotten in the challenge to be the first one home.

My father remained on to rake down the wyndes and tie them firmly with binder twine. I often saw him in the dusk of the evening standing by the gap of a field counting the cocks of hay, the satisfaction of a job well done all around him.

After the work in the meadow was finished the hay was drawn into the barn. We all enjoyed drawing in the hay; there was about it an air of achievement, a fulfilment of the basic need of man to fill the barns and prepare for winter. Next to his family's needs the welfare of his stock was closest to the heart of the farmer and it was every farmer's dread not to have enough to feed his animals in the harsh days of winter. My father had taken on the farm when he was sixteen years old, after the death of my grandfather, and his first winter had come long and harsh and left him with too little hay for the animals. It was a cruel experience for one so young and he never forgot it: at the end of every winter now our barn had a spare block of hay, a monument to my father's hard-earned lesson.

The hay was drawn home in the horse and float – a big sheet of solid timber with two iron wheels and two shafts in front. In the meadow it was tilted up in front so that the back edge lay along the base of the wynde of hay. Then the thick float ropes that were wound around an iron roller at the front of the float were unwound and tied behind the wyndes. The roller was turned, winding up the rope and bringing the cock of hay up along the float. The horse then drew home his load with the driver sitting on the setlock or on top of the wynde, while the children sat along the back of the float, their feet trailing along the fields. Drives in the float were part of their summer entertainment on the farm.

When they arrived in the barn the load was tilted out and, while the man with the horse set off for the next lot, the workers in the barn cleared the way for his return. My father usually piked the hay up and one of us took it from him and passed it back to another who packed it farther back. While the hay in the barn was low the work was very easy, but as the hay rose it became more difficult, and we had to work fast if we wanted to have a rest before the float came back. If the draw was long – coming up from the fields down by the river – we had a nice leisurely time when we could take down the books we had stored on the rafters of the barn. But when the hay was coming from a field near the house, on a hot day and the barn almost full, perspiration ran down your back clogged with dust, hayseeds got into your hair and down your throat, and the break between loads was all too short.

The day the last wynde was drawn home marked the end of the haymaking season. Now the barn was full of soft golden hay, and our animals were safe against the ravages of winter no matter how harsh it might come.

Free To Be Children

Give our children
Time to be children,
To savour the wonder
That is theirs.
To blossom in the world
Of their simplicity,
Not darkened
By the shadows
That are ours.

Let them bask
In the warmth
Of their sunshine,
Cleanse in the
Softness of their tears,
Be kissed by the
Beauties of nature,
Let them be free
In the kingdom
That is theirs.

Their beauty
Is the purity
Of heaven,
Not tainted
By the ugliness
Of man.
Oh, let's not destroy
Their simplicity.
We never can
Improve
On what they have.

Going To Ballybunion

THE HAY IN and the barn full, it was Ballybunion time before the horror of going back to school befell us. The whole family did not go together: my father went by himself after the threshing when Listowel races were on while my mother took the two youngest in August. When we arrived in Ballybunion we checked around in a couple of the guest-houses we usually stayed in, and there were sure to be vacancies in one of them. Some were ordinary guest- houses but others worked an arrangement whereby you bought your own food and they cooked it for you. As they usually had a couple of families staying at the same time, I'm not sure how they sorted it all out.

In the guest-houses we met up with various families, some of whom we knew from previous years. One family I remember was like the steps of stairs, one after the other, and they had a mother who never stopped shouting. At that time there were no wash-hand basins with running water in the bedrooms: instead we had large jugs of water with basins underneath for washing and enamel buckets to hold the used water. One morning this particular family were about to bring their bucket of dirty water down the stairs when they started a fight on the top step. The bucket was turned upside down and rolled down spilling water in all directions: that gave their mother something to shout about!

But the most important job on arriving in Ballybun-ion was to make our way to the "Tricky Tracky" shop for buckets and spades. Tricky Tracky was a marvellous shop full of seaside paraphernalia and it always had a small, brightly coloured merry-go-round twirling in the breeze on the low wall in front of the shop. Then, the first smell of the sea was heaven to our nostrils and we saw the donkey carts with their loads of seaweed trot-ting along the strand. Sunbathing bored us: we climbed rocks and investigated damp eerie caves and packed the long warm day with endless activities. We headed straight for the strand after breakfast and with the exception of mealtimes we never left again till dark.

The headland cliffs of Ballybunion are wild and beautiful but also very dangerous for the unwary. My mother was forever cautioning us about the dangers but her warnings went in one ear and out the other; to us the sea was great fun, where we splashed and dived under waves and got mouths full of salt water. There was a huge cluster of rocks called the Black Rocks which were covered by the full tide but when it was out it left warm pools which sheltered many little sea creatures. We loved investigating all of these and gathering shells and sea grasses. The "Nine Daughters' Hole" was our chamber of horrors: there was a legend attached to it that a man had drowned his nine daughters there because they would not each marry a man of his choice, but I secretly believed that nine daughters were too much for any man and he had gone berserk. We were under severe threat not to go to Nine Daughters' Hole, but of course we did. It was a huge, gaping hole set well back from the edge of the cliffs, but the sea had burrowed its way through the rock at the bottom and thundered in and out with a menacing roar. I always felt the hair rising on the back of my neck as we lay on our stomachs to peer down over the edge. The possibility of slipping brought me out in a cold sweat as I looked down along the sheer black face of the rock at the grey sea belting in and out below.

Sometimes at night – if we promised to behave ourselves – we were taken to the bumpers. Each car took two people but even so they were expensive by our standards and we did not get to go very often. They were inside in a large hall that had other games and kiddy rides, and it was here that I had my first experience of dishonesty. I had a shining silver half-crown which I was keeping in case something special requiring big spending turned up. My father had given it to me before leaving home, and now I took it out of my pocket every so often to savour the thrill of having so much money at my disposal. A big girl began to chat me up with a sad story of having no money because her mother was away and wouldn't be back until the following day: if I gave her my half-crown, she said, she would give it back tomorrow night. My half-crown and I parted company. The next night there was no trace of my new friend and the following night she ran in the other direction as soon as she saw me. It had never dawned on me that she would not give it back, but then the penny dropped. I had lost my half-crown, which was painful, but I also felt let down in a way that was quite new to me.

The old travelling theatre companies were based in Ballybunion for the summer and they brought a new dimension to my thinking: every night a whole new world opened up before my eyes. I soaked in every performance, absorbing the different emotions flowing across the footlights, but the play that made the biggest impression on me was *My Cousin Rachel*. How I suffered with the young wife and resented the black-garbed, threatening housekeeper! However, the one who really got to me was the leading man, who stole my heart away. It was the first yelp of puppy love and I wallowed in its agony and ecstacy.

My mother spent her days sitting on a rug in a sunny cove where she met up with many old friends. Ballybunion at that time was the holiday centre for Cork, Kerry and Limerick, so she met far-flung relations and "connections". She was the only person whom I ever heard use that word: it meant somebody whose family was connected to yours by marriage. There was no blood relationship but they were still in her calculation on the outer fringes of the family circle. She loved talking to people and she would listen to the most boring old crones for hours on end and sympathize with all their sad stories. But she met some great characters as well. I remember one happy fat lady who never had a swimming suit and used to go into the sea in an overflowing bra and big pink knickers. She swam like a giant fish and would carry you so far out to sea that you had to sink or swim. Another great source of entertainment was the sight of pot-bellied men and large-bottomed women; bare flesh got rare exposure in Ireland at that time. Listening to these strangers, we found the Kerry accent soft and caressing but the Limerick people had a way of saying "Are you here for a forthnight?" that we would mimic endlessly.

For the entire two weeks in Ballybunion we never wore shoes except when going to church, to which my mother dragged us protesting every morning for Mass. She thought it was marvellous to be able to get daily Mass but we did not think that it was so great; however, the strand and the sea at that time of morning looked calm and peaceful and it felt good to run down and be the first to leave your footprints along the wide expanse of golden sand. My mother visited the church at night as well to say her rosary, but when I got bored I would leave her at it and ramble off outside. Religion, I discovered, could be very time-consuming. Across from the church was a wide area of waste ground overgrown with weeds and briars, and strangely enough right in the middle of it was a bright red flower. I sat on the wall and imagined all sorts of fantasies about that flower: in one I was an orphan on a desert island who turned into a red flower. My mother praying gave me plenty of time to dream.

At the end of the holidays we came home bronzed and my fair hair was always white from the sun. We were ready but reluctant to face back to school.

A Memory

The waste ground was choked with weeds
They grew above her head
But in the middle of this waste
One flower of golden red.

The little child came every day
To gaze upon this scene
The flower it was the loveliest sight
That she had ever seen.

This flower took root and blossomed
It grew inside her head
And led her on to lovely things
Long after it was dead.

To School Through The Fields

GOING TO SCHOOL and coming back was so enjoyable that it made school itself bearable. My main objection to school was that I had to stay there: it was the first experience to interfere with my freedom and it took me a long time to accept that there was no way out of its trap. I could look out through a window in the back wall of the schoolhouse and see my home away in the distance, with the fields stretching out invitingly and with the Darigle river glinting in the valley. I made many an imaginary journey home through that window: it was not that I wished to be at home so much, but that I wanted to be free to ramble out through the fields. I envied the freedom of the crows on the trees outside the window, coming and going as they pleased.

But school became an accepted pattern and even though it had its black days it had its good ones as well. The black days were mainly in winter when we arrived through the fields with sodden boots and had to sit in the freezing cold with a harsh wind whipping in under the door and up through the floorboards. The school was an old stone building with tall rattling windows and black cobweb-draped rafters, and when the wind howled the whole school groaned and creaked. The floor had large gaping holes through which an occasional rat peeped up to join the educational circle.

The educational process of the day was based on repetition: we repeated everything so often that it *had* to penetrate into our uninterested minds. A booster, by way of a sharp slap across the fingers with a hazel rod, sharpened our powers of perception. Learning was not optional and the sooner you learnt that fact, the freer from conflict life became. All the same, most of the teachers were as kind as the system allowed them to be, but inspectors breathed down their necks and after them came the priests to check our religious knowledge. One stern-faced priest peered down at me from his six-foot height when I was in third class and demanded to know: "What is transubstantiation?"

Education was certainly not child oriented but our way of life compensated for its shortcomings. Sometimes, though unaware of it, we tried to educate our teachers, especially the ones that came from nearby towns to do part-time duty. One of these asked us to write a composition on "Life on the Farm". I loved writing compositions and my problem was not how to start but how to finish. I included in my account a description of the sex life of a cow and when I got my copy back from the teacher this section was ringed with a red pencil. A red mark meant an error so I checked every word for spelling in my dictionary but found nothing wrong. I returned to school the following day to ask the teacher what was wrong.

"That sentence should be left out," she said.

"But why?" I asked.

"It's not suitable," she answered, giving me a strange look.

On returning home in a very confused state I explained my problem to my mother. She read my composition, smiled and said: "People from a different background do not always understand". It took me another couple of years to understand why the teacher did not understand.

Ours was a mixed school and this suited everybody because families and neighbours were not split up but could all go to school together. The boys played football at one side of the yard and the girls played hunt and cat and mouse at the other side. At the back of the school the boys' and girls' toilets, which consisted of a timber bench with a circle cut in it to facilitate bottoms of all sizes, were separated by a stone wall. The little toilet building was partly roofed with galvanised but this had grown to a complete roof by years of free-growing ivy.

The school had just two rooms. The master had a room to himself and the second room was shared by the two other teachers: one taught infants and first class at one side of the room, while second and third classes were taught by the second teacher at the other side. It was open plan education and if you got bored at your end you could tune in to the other side, at the risk of a slap across the ear if you were caught out.

We ate our lunch, which consisted of a bottle of milk and two slices of home-made brown bread, sitting on a grassy ditch around the school, and we fed the crumbs to the birds. In winter the milk bottles were heated around the fire during classes, often resulting in corks popping from the heat and, if the cork could not pop because it was screwed on we had a mini-explosion and a milk lake.

There was a cottage near the school from which we collected a pot of tea each day for the teachers, and this provided a welcome diversion, especially in summer. We went down a narrow lane which led into a long garden abounding with rows of vegetables, fruit trees and flowers. These flowers overflowed onto the paths and climbed up over the windows and onto the thatched roof of the cottage: it was almost buried in flowers, and when you went down the steps and through the doorway you stepped into another world. Inside the cottage was shadowed and had an air of mystery because every available space seemed to be filled with the treasures of the old couple who lived there. All around was the smell of flowers and on the table were bowls of fresh fruit from the garden. When you arrived into the kitchen you were seated on a soft *súgán* chair and given a cup of scalding tea coloured with goat's milk and a cut of bread with a thick layer of homemade jam, and afterwards you got a fistful of strawberries or raspberries that were soft and luscious. The little window on the back wall of the cottage was frilled with a lace curtain tied back with a ribbon and through the sparkling glass you could see the back garden as profuse and colourful as the front. It was a dream cottage and John O' and Mrs O' were ideal occupants. They were gentle people; she wore a long skirt with her hair coiled in a soft roll on top of her head, he was a neat little man with a black moustache, and always wore a navy suit. The trip to John O's cottage brightened up many a school day tinged with monotony.

Going to school in the winter mornings through the grey frosty fields had its own beauty. The bushes and briars took on unearthly shapes of frozen rigidity and the trees glittered with outstretched arms like graceful ballerinas; underfoot the grass crunched beneath our strong leather boots. The muddy gaps through which the cows waded up to their knees in gutter were now strangely transformed into frozen masses of intriguing shapes. In their frozen state you could dance from one strange pattern formation to another or try to crack the black ice with the tipped heel of your boot and create your own strange designs. This grey frozen land was much more interesting and comfortable than its rain-soaked winter companion. In the rain you could slip on the wet grass and have a wet bottom to sit on for the day or, going through the gaps between the fields, an unwary step could land you with two boots full of mud and water. We had two glaises to contend with; these were waterways larger and rougher than streams but smaller than rivers. Now swollen with floods they provided an additional hazard and we crossed them on stepping stones while the brown foaming water swirled around our boots. I had mental images of slipping off the stones and being carried by the rushing water down to the river that was roaring through the valley below, but somehow we survived all these winter threats and they added a sense of adventure to making it through the fields every day.

Summer came at last. We welcomed it and the freedom it brought from the shackles of winter. When the warm days were firmly established we kicked off our heavy boots and long black stockings and danced through the warm grass in delight, the morning fields moist with dew that ran down our bare legs and trickled between our toes. Cobwebs sparkled on the bushes and cascaded onto the grass, joining the fields and ditches in a shimmering web. The sun warmed us and set our journey aglow. The day in school was just an unwelcome interlude then between the morning trek and the return home, and if the journey to school took about thirty minutes, the coming home could take anything up to two hours.

On leaving school we ran down the lane and over a wooden fence into a large hilly field. We ran around in circles flinging our sacks ahead of us and running after them, like young calves kicking up their heels at the first taste of freedom in an open field. Half way down that field was a small well in the side of a mossy ditch with a grey timber gate covering it. This was John O's well and the gate was to keep his goat away from it, so the goat had to content himself with the stream outside.

This was our first stop. Here we collapsed on the warm grass and stretched out in the sun. We swapped stories, one more far-fetched than the last, and one of the boys sometimes made pools in the well stream for the birds to bathe in. He loved the birds and they reciprocated his feeling because they showed no fear of him.

Then we washed our lunch bottles and filled them with cold spring water and, having drunk enough, we refilled them for the safari home. We ran to the bottom of the hill and in under the overhanging trees where our first glaise tumbled over green mossy stones. Here, if the humour was on us, we might block up a large pool and paddle in and out of it, hitching up our skirts by tucking them up the legs of our knickers. The boys had short pants, but they rolled them up further, revealing patches of white above their mahogany brown knees. Tiring of this we rambled along the next field which led to the only stretch of road on the journey home, a short bit of road made up mainly of a long stone bridge. Under this bridge the Darigle river hid itself between deep grassy banks, and sometimes we went over the low wall of the bridge to catch collies. Other evenings we hung over the bridge watching the water-hens darting in and out beneath the bank. The hens' hatching time was eagerly observed and the evening the chicks appeared was as exciting as the arrival of a new baby at home.

It was difficult to drag ourselves away from there, but leaving the road we parted with some of our friends and took to the fields again. Rambling on through two more glens we came to another glaise, which was covered with briars and bushes. We burrowed underneath them and splashed into the cool green water before climbing up a stone ditch at the other side. Now came our greatest test of strength: a steep hill which we zigzagged up very slowly, stopping half way to replenish our strength with our water bottles. Finally we reached the top where we sat down for a long time to finish our bottles. From this hilltop perch we looked back over the valley we had just come through and the school looked small in the distance, which felt most satisfactory. We watched the different herds of cows grazing and picked out the bulls. These were something to be reckoned with constantly on our journey to and from school: some were killers and had to be kept at a safe distance, which often necessitated putting extra fields between us and them. We recognized their different roars and checked every field to make sure of their whereabouts.

Having recovered from our hill climb we often picked buttercups and made daisy chains. Then, as we sauntered on through the remaining fields, we checked our birds' nests to see how things were progressing. An odd time we met one of the neighbours and if we were lucky got invited in for a cup of milk and currant cake. The last few fields were flat and mossy and we picked blackberries or sometimes, when they were in season, we filled our bottles with black sloes and buried them to make sloe wine – only we could never remember afterwards where we had hidden them. Finally we arrived home sun-soaked and relaxed, with school almost forgotten because it was, after all, only one part of a much larger cycle of education.

A School Friend

We walked to school
Through the dew drenched fields
Meeting where our paths crossed
At the foot of a grassy hill.
If one ran late, the other
Left a stone message
On the mossy bridge.
He had muddy boots,
A jumper torn by briars
And hair that went its own way.
Trivial details to a mind
That raced amongst the clouds
And followed rabbits down brown burrows.
Gentle hands, twisted by a bad burning,
Reached out towards the birds,
And they perched on his fingers
At ease with one of their own.
Blessed with a mind that ran free
From the frailties of his body
He walked during his quiet life
Close to the gates of heaven.

Our Daily Bread

THE DAY ON the farm started at about 7.00 a.m. with a quick cup of tea. Then, when the cows had been milked and my father had gone to the creamery, the rest of us sat down to a long, leisurely breakfast. Preparations for dinner meant going to the field where the potatoes and vegetables grew and digging a bucket of potatoes and cutting some heads of cabbage; a big black pot of potatoes was boiled every day and whatever was left went with the other scraps to feed the farm dogs and the pigs. Dinner itself was at one o'clock, and a shrill iron whistle that hung beside the kitchen door summoned us: we could hear it fields away. At four o'clock we had afternoon tea, and whatever time the cows were milked in the evening was supper time.

The evening milking was a restful moment in the day. Men and women, tired after their work, slapped their little milking stools on the ground beside the cows. We called the stool "the block", maybe because it consisted of a two-inch block of solid timber with three legs broadening out at the base to give balance. Having made sure that your block was secure, you sat down with a bucket between your knees and rested your forehead against the soft, silken flank of the cow. Then, wrapping your fingers around the cow's warm teats, you milked to a steady, soothing rhythm. At first the milk hit the tin bucket with a sharp metallic sound but as it filled it mellowed to a drowsy hum and the cold bucket grew warm between your legs.

Milking time was singing time; it was debating time if your fellow milkers felt so inclined; or it could be just dreaming time. If, however, the cow felt that her presence was being ignored she could draw a sharp kick and send you sprawling into the centre channel of the stalls, baptizing you with the bucket of warm milk. Most were tranquil animals but we had a few of what my father called "kickers". Each cow had a name and the kicking strain could follow from mother to daughter, and often we had a mother and daughter in the one herd.

The cows were of many different strains and colours; specialization had not yet come in. We had a family called "Legs": these were long-legged white cows; and the white cows were termed "baney". There was a strain of small brown ones we called "Mouse", and we had both a mother Mouse and a young Mouse; I liked the mother Mouse particularly because she was so quiet and easygoing and never kicked.

We carried the buckets full of milk to the churns, which we called "tanks", on the stand outside the stalls, and around the top of each tank was a muslin cloth through which we strained the milk. When Dan was staying he rather than my father might sometimes take the milk to the creamery; however, this occasionally led to problems. These were the early days of hygiene inspectors and Dan resented inspectors in any form: he absolutely refused to allow any inspection of our tanks, demanding to know of them,

"What did you ever do for your country that entitled you to go around smelling our milk?"

After such an altercation a hurried SOS would come from the creamery to channel Dan in another direction.

In early spring or late autumn when milk production was at its lowest we separated our own milk and made butter. We poured the milk, still warm from the cow, into the separator – a large iron dish with two pipes, which was attached to a motor with a handle. It gave off a soft whine when the handle was turned, and out of one pipe came cream, out of the other skim-milk. It was a simple but ingenious device and while my father manned it we young ones lined up with cups for drinks of cream.

On the following day the cream was put into the churn to make butter. We had two churns: a hand one which sat on a table and could be worked by one person and a barrel churn which stood on a stand and required two churners, though if woman power was scarce, which seldom happened, one could manage it. After a certain amount of churning the thick cream formed into lumps of butter. The faster one could achieve this the better the butter, and this was the source of the country saying that "Long churning makes bad butter", a saying which was considered applicable to many situations in life. The butter made, it was washed and salted; what remained in the churn was buttermilk, a grand drink on a hot summer day and a great favourite of the men coming in from the fields.

The crops we had planted in spring grew through the summer months and as they ripened the differences between them became evident: the wheat was a golden brown, the oats a butter yellow, and the barley with its bearded head the old man of the three. Cutting the corn in the autumn meant the winding down of the year's work, and it was a task in which the neighbours came together and helped each other out. When the corn had been cut and bound into sheaves, stooks were made and finally handstacks; then the handstacks were drawn home with the horse and float and the different ricks (or "reeks" as we called them) were made.

The threshing was one of the biggest events of the

farming year; the sowing of the seeds in the spring, followed by the cutting of the corn, were all a build-up to this point. Now the wheat would be threshed into grain, which would in turn be ground into flour to give us our daily bread.

Coming home from school through the fields we heard the hum of the thresher in the different farmyards and counted the days until it would pull into our haggard. Finally, on coming home one evening, we would be told that the threshing machine was coming to our farm that night. We waited in the haggard and kept our ears strained for the sound of the old engine, our eyes peeled for the sight of the smoke above the trees. Living still in the age of the horse, anything motorised that moved on wheels on the farm was to us a kind of miracle.

At last we heard the engine grumbling its way along and saw the high, pink-timbered threshing machine between the hedges; as I watched it coming down the laneway I felt thrills of anticipation shooting out through my toes. Getting the long, unwieldy paraphernalia into the haggard was a slow and complicated ordeal and it was a great place to be if you wanted to learn any new curses. The greasy overalled engine men twisted and manoeuvred this iron monster which all the time belched smoke and spluttered in protest. Finally, after much discussion and pacing of distances, the most suitable position was achieved: she was set and ready for action the following morning.

After breakfast the engine was coaxed into life and as it coughed and finally roared it sent out smoke signals that brought the men from miles around. They came from across the river, down from the hill, across the fields and down the laneway. They were weather-beaten, work-hardened men and each one carried a pike; they came at a lively pace with a hunger for work in their stride.

OUR DAILY BREAD

The threshing was a test of working skills in which men showed their mettle and, even though they often worked hard days at home, they did not always have such an audience. It was also one of the most sociable days of the year, for some of these men met only at threshings and so had a year's events to discuss. Some of them opened the reek and threw the sheaves to those on top of the thresher. At the back of the thresher where the straw poured out was one of the toughest jobs in piking away the straw. Here a reek of straw was made, and as the reek of corn reduced in size this rose higher; there was skill in making a well balanced reek.

The story of the harvest was told at the front of the thresher. Here the golden grain poured out of little trap doors into jute bags. This was where my father took control: he scooped up the first grains anxiously into his fist and examined them on the palm of his hand; then he put a few into his mouth and chewed them thoughtfully with his eyes closed. He was like a connoisseur sampling wine as he tested his year's work. Finally, he opened his eyes and, rubbing his hands together, declared: "Great stuff, that".

It was lovely to watch the gold grain pour into the nut-brown bags. When it was about four inches from the top we quickly changed bags; then the full bags were carried on the backs of the men across the haggard to the loft, a long, low stone building with a timber floor. The grain was poured from the open bags onto the floor, starting at the back wall. As the bags were open-mouthed on their backs the men just bent forward without removing them and the grain poured out over their shoulders. I helped my father switching the bags at the mouth of the thresher and a sense of togetherness and harmony with the satisfaction of a job well done built up between us during the day.

All that day the thresher droned and the men worked

103

steadily, breaking only for dinner and tea. It took large supplies to feed the hungry *meitheal* (the group of neighbours who had come to work with us) and if Napoleon believed that an army marched on its stomach my mother believed that the threshing men worked on theirs. There was an air of good fellowships and fun both in the haggard and around the kitchen table. At the side of the thresher a large pile of chaff – featherlight bits of straw and empty ears of corn – built up and here, after school, the neighbouring children played, burrowing into it and throwing it at each other while the men shouted at them to get out of the way. The haggard was the realm of the men and children to which the women, busy in the kitchen, rarely came.

Gradually, as the reeks of corn disappeared and the reeks of straw towered high, the threshing wound down; we children were sorry to hear it shuddering to a halt. Then the men helped to get the thresher and engine out, a complicated business because the wheels were so heavy that sometimes they sank into the soft ground. After much pushing and shunting she finally got going and it was with a sense of sadness that I watched the whole gangling procession steam its way up the passage. The top-heavy thresher frequently swayed at precarious angles but always recovered in time to right itself.

The threshing was over for another year and the men went home to their various farms to milk the cows, their children with them. The haggard, a hue of different shades of yellow and brown, was silent at last. The bright yellow straw, the soft yellow chaff and the rich dark earth where the wheels of the thresher had cut. My father stood with one hand on his hip and the other rubbing the base of his neck: it was his stance when everything was right in his world. He walked to the open door of the loft where the rich-coloured grain spread out in waves to the four corners. I stood beside him, silent lest I break the magic of his moment of inner peace. He was a man who was often aggravated by some of the aspects of farming, but at times like this he reached a high plateau of fulfilment, and later he and my mother would go together to view the loft.

When the geese and ducks arrived back for the night from the fields there were shrieks of joy, for the haggard after threshing was a haven of rare delight for them. They screeched and they quacked and they tore into the chaff with all the sounds of ecstasy. They ate it, they burrowed into in, and they rolled over in it: such was their harvest thanksgiving.

Later some of the grain was taken to the mill for crushing. A large quantity of the oats was left as it was to be fed to the hens and horses. The crushed oats and barley were used to feed the pigs and some of the cows, and the wheat was milled for flour. Some of the wheat was sold and more returned for our own use. My mother baked every day: big circles of brown and white bread baked in the bastables over the fire. Shop bread rarely appeared on our table. She made big currant cakes and apple cakes with the apples from our own orchard. We had huge old apple trees that produced an abundance of fruit which my mother stored in boxes in the loft; they seldom had time to dry out as our consumption was heavy and demand always exceeded supply. After a stormy night the pigs had a feast in the orchard eating the windfalls, but when my brother started beekeeping the hives were under the apple trees and the pigs were forced out. They resented this infringement of their rights but when they made any attempt to force an entrance the bees went on the attack. I often saw the herd, with tails curled high, screeching in protest and running as fast as their short legs would carry them.

A Rusty Love Affair

In a sun-baked shed
With black grained hands
These iron men of steam
Sweat oil pursuing an ideal.
There she sits in state,
This queen of the past,
Waiting for her archaic
Limbs to be greased
Into motion, her joints
Soothed gently by her
Black lovers, unquestioning
In their complete adoration.
In this brown station yard
Carriages grey with old age,
Retired queens, proudly wear
The grandeur of another day.
Here, a dream in creation,
An old train being reborn
When men become gods
Breathing life into dead iron.

My Father's Butter Box

IN OUR LOCAL creamery butter was stored in solid boxes, about two and a half feet wide, made of fine timber with a yellow waxen sheen. Many found their ways into local farmers' houses where they were put to good use; one such was the butter box that came into our house and became my father's tool box.

It had lost its former waxen elegance and had turned a muddy brown, with a bit missing off the top at one side. Into this my father had collected a miscellaneous assortment of hammers, wrenches and screwdrivers, together with nails, washers and screws of varying degrees of antiquity. On top came bits of timber and rubber and all kinds of odds and ends left over from previous jobs. He never threw anything away in case it might come in handy in the future, but this practice was self-defeating as he could never find anything he wanted. His box was packed full to the very top and had to be dragged rather than lifted due to its immense weight.

When he had a job to do out came the butter box. The jobs could vary from putting a handle on a brush to replacing a window or fixing the leg of a chair that was unable to withstand our daily assaults. The butter box was an essential part of these undertakings. At first my father dug and poked into its depths looking for a nail of the required length. Many were discarded in a rising tide of frustration and annoyance at their unsuitability until eventually, in a final crescendo of pure anger, the whole box was turned upside down on the kitchen floor. Ours was a large kitchen but when my father's box was upended its contents scattered to the four walls with screws and nails rolling under all the presses and chairs. As most of the contents of the box had rusted to various shades of brown over the years, our kitchen now took on the appearance of a ploughed field. At this stage the whole house came to a standstill while my father poured a tirade of colourful language on the head of any nail that had the audacity to bend before reaching its prescribed destination. His favourite expression when he had reached the limits of his endurance was "hoor's bastard!" and when I was young I thought that a "hoor's bastard" was a crooked nail and that a "hoor" was a cow who would refuse to go through a gateway when my father intended that she should.

The job, depending on the size of the undertaking, could go on for many hours during which time we children ran back and forth answering his every demand and sometimes anticipating them like a team of nurses tending a surgeon during a major operation. I will say one thing for this exercise: it certainly sharpened our reflexes and if the hammer slipped and he hit his thumb instead of the nail we heard adjectives hitherto unknown to us. Finally the mission was accomplished and our carpenter downed tools. He then found other more important things to attend to and walked away leaving chaos behind. It was our job to pick up every single item and throw it in the butter box, and this we did with a vengeance so that the final state of the box was worse than the first, thus guaranteeing another performance at a later date. The cleaning up was a slow, laborious, monotonous job and we hated every minute of it, though it was surely a great training in the development of patience. When the kitchen floor was finally brushed and the last bit of rubbish shovelled into the butter box, the floor which was normally a stone grey was now a symphony of browns and greens of sufficient variety to thrill the heart of any landscape artist.

My mother, a wise woman, was seldom in the kitchen for these performances. This was not by chance but part of her marital strategy. She was very happily married for over forty years to a man who was an excellent husband but whose threshold of tolerance was very low. She thus avoided direct confrontation and quietly out-manoeuvred him, believing that in marriage, as in battle, strategy was of all importance.

In after years my father's butter box became a joke in our family and we often wondered how he would have fitted into a modern semi-detached in suburbia with an equal-rights wife and modern teenagers. He was never designed for "little boxes" living.

The Last Litany

DESPITE THE FACT that my mother was tolerant and flexible in most situations, she did have streaks of uncompromising rigidity. The family rosary was one of these: sick, maimed or crippled, we were all on our knees for the rosary, and helpers, visitors, or anyone who happened to call at the wrong time were apt to be included.

During the summer months I knelt inside the kitchen window looking down over the fields where the cows were grazing after milking. When my turn came to give out the decade I used the cows in the field to count my ten Hail Marys. I mentally sectioned off ten in a corner, but as my mind floated back and forth across the valley the cows naturally moved around so my ten could decrease to five or six. If I said the Glory before schedule my mother gently intervened in the background – "Two more". Or if my herd increased and my Hail Marys swelled beyond the ten she interrupted with "Glory, now, Glory". She also fought gallantly to keep us all supplied with rosary beads but they were continually getting lost or broken. She never tried to convert my father to beads, so he cracked his knuckles as he went along to keep count.

Her rosary was one thing, but her additions to it were something else. First came the litany starting "Holy Mary", and we would all chant, "Pray for us" in response.

110

After Holy Mary came a long list and somewhere down along the list came "Ark of the Covenant" and "Gate of Heaven". After "Gate of Heaven" one night my mother lost her concentration and she floundered and repeated it a few times, failing to remember what came next. Finally a little voice in the background piped up helpfully: "Try Nelson's Pillar!" Everybody fell around the floor laughing, and my father took advantage of the opportunity to call a halt to the litany for the night.

But the litany was only one of the many additions. There were three Hail Marys for this neighbour and a second lot for another one, until my father would start complaining, "For God's sake, we'll be here till morning". We prayed diligently for years for one neighbour who was studying to be a teacher and of whom my father voiced the opinion that "if a bumble bee had his brains he'd fly backwards", but despite this pronouncement on the neighbour's grey matter he still qualified. It was my mother's conviction that prayer could move mountains and indeed hers often did; at least they moved mountains of ignorance. During exam time she always lit a candle in the centre of the parlour table. I would come home during exams and peep into the parlour to check if she had remembered. It was always lighting. It was a symbol of caring and in later years her children wrote as adults to her from many corners of the world asking her to light her candle and pray for their special problems.

She had an implicit faith in the goodness and power of God but despite this she was always late for Mass. If left to her own devices she would never have made it at all, but my father was a punctuality addict. He was ready half an hour before time and paced up and down the kitchen floor ranting and swearing; then he would go to the kitchen door and, scratching his head and raising his eyes towards heaven, would declare: "If ever a

111

man suffered!" I think that he was imploring God to witness that this was his agony in the garden. Finally he would stand at the foot of the stairs and shout: "Missus, is it today or next Sunday we're going to Mass?" Normally he called my mother Len, but if she was pushing him to the limits of his endurance it changed to "missus": this was his signal to her that thus far and no further could she go. Finally she arrived, pulling on her hat and calling instructions back over her shoulder to those staying at home. She was only going to be missing for a few hours, but a stranger could be forgiven for thinking that a world voyage was on the agenda.

Organized planning and good housekeeping were not on the top of her list of priorities and it was to people she gave her number one commitment. She always had time to listen and chat. If you ever had to leave the house very early in the morning she was there. She was with you having the breakfast to listen to any worries troubling you; late at night she was in the kitchen waiting to have a cup of tea. She never told us that she loved us but she wrapped us in blankets of love and did not need to use words. Her love and serenity filled the house and she herself was one of the most contented people I ever knew. In an era when corporal punishment was the rule of the day she did not believe in smacking children; she maintained that slapping them made children bold and aggressive. One day I came home from school to find a stream of water pouring out the door against me. She was baby-sitting a neighbour's little girl, an only child who was always beautifully dressed, and in the middle of the kitchen she had a wheelbarrow full of sand and water; not a little wheelbarrow mind you, but a large, rusty, iron model. When I asked her the reason for the wheelbarrow I was informed that it was good for children to make a mess and that sand and water was of great benefit to them.

THE LAST LITANY

She absolutely forbade bad language from any of us children, and though my father indulged in all sorts of colourful phrases it was accepted that it was his prerogative and did not extend to the rest of us. She amazed me in later years by quite blandly informing me that my father used only the words necessary to describe any given situation, and she was quite right.

Togetherness

Forced apart
By busy days
We who belong
Together
As the interlaced
Fingers
Of praying
Hands
Join again
In quite times
At peace
In our
Togetherness

The Cut-Throat
Nuns

W E LIVED ABOUT three miles from the nearest
town but the passage, as we called it, from the
road to our home was another half a mile. On
each side of the passage from the gateway were high
mossy ditches where birds and rabbits nestled, and
further down were seven gates marking the divisions
between the fields as this was also the access lane for
the cattle and machinery going along the farm. Lorry
drivers dreaded our farm and one cranky individual
once poked his head out of his cab at my father and
demanded: "Does the Almighty God know that people
live down here?"

I loved walking down that laneway and I knew every
twig and branch along the way. The first time that the
joy of returning home along it hit me was after my first
enforced absence from home, when I had to go into hospital in Cork for a week to have my tonsils removed.
The prospect had not worried me greatly to begin with;
however, when I had seen my mother's hat disappearing
out the hospital gate I had begun to feel abandoned,
and the week that had followed was to put me off hospi-
tals and nuns for the rest of my life. The nuns in their
virginal white habits sailed around the wards like bil-
lowing swans and, when the operation left my throat
feeling as if the French guillotine had done a job on it,
I discovered that their snowy white exterior penetrated

115

to their inner regions as well, for the nuns treated us with cool efficiency but with very little of the milk of human kindness. I do not think that they believed in the approach expressed in "suffer little children to come unto Me".

At home whenever one of us had a sore throat my mother soaked bread in warm milk and this remedy slid down a raw throat like soft butter. Now in hospital my throat screamed in agony with every swallow and my stomach groaned because its food supply was cut off. I thought with longing of my mother's solution: we called it "goody", a childish word and, like most children's expressions, an apt description. But when I asked one of the nuns if she had ever heard of "goody" she threw back her head, gave a braying laugh like our jennet when he had been tied up for too long and, looking around the ward, she asked in a high, nasal voice: "Did any of you ever hear of 'goody'?" She pronounced it as if it were a dirty word, and I wished that I could have used some of my father's favourite phrases to tell her what I thought of her.

The week in that hospital was a bewildering experience. The babies in the ward cried all the time they were awake; it was the era of restricted visiting and the children cried from loneliness. At home on the farm we cuddled our baby animals when they were sick: here in hospital these children fared far worse and it was heart-breaking to see the little tear-stained faces peering through the iron bars of the cots.

After a few days, when I had begun to recover and to get my bearings, I began to plan my escape. Nobody, I decided, could survive in this set-up for very long. Across the road from the hospital was a hotel. I sat on the verandah outside the children's ward and watched the comings and goings at the hotel hoping to see a familiar face, and finally I spotted an old friend of my father's. The next day I watched my chance to make my way out the front door of the hospital and I shouted across at Jack when he appeared. I poured out my troubles to him, and discovered that he was going home by bus that evening. I asked him to call for me on his way to the bus; then I went back to the nuns and told them that my father was collecting me that evening. Eventually they relented and agreed to let me go. I felt like somebody released from jail after serving a sentence of hard labour. As we travelled to Lisnasheoga the engine of the bus was happily singing "Going Home".

As I opened the gate of the road to our farm I felt such a surge of joy pour over me that I could have flown over the fields. I sat on a stone and my eyes roved over every familiar detail of that view; in the haze of the late summer evening it looked serene and welcoming. I was so glad to be home.

That was my first experience of a deep-rooted love of the very fields of home. Every evening my father would walk these fields, checking the animals and seeing that everything was as it should be. It was not actually necessary to do this every day but he enjoyed walking the fields – you were never alone in them, with the farm animals and the wildlife all around you. At that time there was a lovely practice known as blessing the crops: these were days of supplication when God was asked to bless the harvest. The farmer went to every field with a bottle of holy water, and he sprinkled the holy water and said whatever prayers he thought suitable, giving special attention to those fields in which crops were planted. I accompanied both my father and my mother as they did this, and I felt a great sense of harmony, a blending of man, nature and God in complete unity.

Yalla Bacon

WE KILLED TWO pigs every year for our household needs. On the day of the killing my father acted as butcher and the neighbours as fellow executioners. A big timber table was scrubbed white and beside it a timber barrel of boiling water was placed in readiness, and these were positioned outside the old, disused turf house. The pig was then led to the slaughter, but you could not say that he came like a lamb: he fought every step of the way. It took four strong men to hold him down on the table until my father, with the expertise born of years of practice, brought the whole drama to a speedy conclusion with his long, deadly, butcher's knife, while my mother held the white enamel bucket into which the warm red blood gushed forth. When the killing was taking place I stayed upstairs with my head under a pillow; I could not bear to see my friends meet their death.

Once dead the pigs were scalded in the barrel of boiling water, washed and shaved clean of hair. Then they were hung by the back legs from the rafters of the turf house, slit down the lengths of their bellies and their insides removed. Then my mother set to work, sorting every bit of the pig into her white enamel bath and buckets. Very little was discarded. The insides of the pig were then washed down with buckets of water that ran out the door and into the stream outside. When the cleaning was complete three ash rods, peeled and pointed, were used to keep the sides apart: one at the shoulder, one at the ham and the third in the middle. The turf house door was then shut and bolted. I used to peep in through the slits in the timber door to see the two white carcasses hanging in the semi-darkness and I felt very much in awe of these ghost-like figures.

They hung there for two days, during which time my mother was preparing for filling the puddings. First the puddings were washed and re-washed so many times that our fingers would be numb from cold water. The final washings were done in spring water from the fairy well and this water, because it came straight from the bowels of the earth, was ice cold on even the hottest day. When the puddings were snow white they were left soaking in a bath of spring water, and looked like a nest of slithering eels. The lard was removed from the pig and rendered down in the bastable until it was clear liquid; then it was poured into an enamel bucket where it formed a solid block which was used for cooking and frying. When the fat was run off left in the oven were the graves – bits of gristle and meat that were embedded in the fat and would not melt – that were later minced for the puddings. My mother cooked the pig's blood and liver and many other bits and pieces that only she could identify.

When everything was cooked and in readiness, filling the puddings would commence. All the meats were put in the mincer, herbs and spices were added, and once the mincing was completed a filler was attached to the mincer. We filled white and black puddings; the basis of the black ones was the pig's blood and the white ones minced belly meat and breadcrumbs. A huge black pot of boiling water bubbled over the fire and as soon as each ring of pudding was complete and tied firmly it was plunged into the boiling water. As the pudding cooked an aromatic smell filled the kitchen; it was then lifted out of the pot using a clean handle of a brush and rested across the backs of two chairs where the steaming puddings gave off a mouth-watering fragrance. Row after row of puddings replaced each other on the brush handle, enough to feed an army and, in fact, because all the neighbours got a supply, there was almost a small army to be fed.

The salting of the pig took place the second night after the killing. As soon as darkness fell that night all the neighbours came to help with the work. The backbones were removed from the pigs and they were brought into the kitchen in four sides of pork. First they were cut into sections large enough for our daily needs and then the salting began. A big jute bag of salt sat in the middle of the kitchen floor between the two tables on which the pigs were being salted and we children distributed it in basins to the men who rubbed it into the meat and under the bones. Then the meat was packed between layers of salt in a big wooden barrel which was later filled with fresh spring water. The pork steak, backbone, and some choice pieces were left free of salt.

When the work was finished the tables were scrubbed and the kitchen tidied, the bastable put over the fire and filled with pork steak. The two tables were set for a late supper and when the steak was golden brown we had platefuls of it with tea and brown bread. The following day we went around to all the neighbours with pork steak, fresh pork and puddings – and they did likewise when they killed their pigs. We had the homemade puddings for breakfast, dinner and supper while they lasted; the backbone roasted was a tasty dish, and the pig's ear was grilled over the open fire. Even the pig's bladder was used; seasoned up the chimney and then pumped up to become next season's football. Every last scrap of the animal was put to use.

If my mother could get away with it she hid some of the puddings, which she hung up the chimney to be smoked. Gradually we ate our way down that barrel of bacon: we had bacon and cabbage, bacon and turnips, and once or twice a year – when my mother decided that the iron in nettles was very good for us – we had bacon and nettles, which we ate under loud protest. The remaining bacon was taken out of the barrel and hung off the hooks in the rafters of the kitchen, where it turned a golden yellow from the smoke of the open fire. If real smoked ham was required the bacon was hung up the chimney, which had ample accommodation in its cavernous interior.

Practically all the meat we ate was produced on our own farm. My mother reared and fattened chickens which she boiled and roasted; we also had roast duck and, on festive occasions, roast goose or turkey. Trout was a regular Sunday dish and, as my father also liked to shoot, pheasant sometimes came our way.

In the autumn the potatoes were picked and drawn home from the field. They were then stored in the potato pit, a six foot-long trench that was about two feet deep and three feet wide. Butt loads of potatoes were poured into it and stacked high, and then thatched with straw to ward off the rain and frost. The turnips and mangles were treated in like manner. The turnips were for kitchen use while the mangles, chopped up in a machine called a pulper, were fed to the horses and the pigs. The pig was the waste disposal unit of the farmyard and ate anything that came his way. Any heads of cabbage still remaining in the fields were cut and brought home to be fed to the cows because cabbage, unlike the other vegetables, could not be stored over the winter. And so the fields were cleared of crops and when the weather got cold the cattle were also brought off the land, back to the farmyard, where they slept in their comfortable straw-filled houses at night and went out during the day for water and exercise in a field near the house.

The turf was drawn home from the bog and built into a rick behind the house. The turf house was also filled to the door and here what we called brus, the broken up sods of turf, formed on the floor over the following weeks. This brus was used for lighting the fire, with little bits of kindling which we collected from under the trees in the groves and the fort.

At the beginning of winter a mountain of logs was stacked high beside the house. We were surrounded by trees and when some were brought down by storms they were cut up with a large saw called the cross-cut which was worked by two men. Then they were split with the sledge and wedges, and finally chopped smaller with the hatchet. I loved sitting on the pile of freshly cut logs, running my hands over the different shapes and smelling their woody fragrance. To this day I think that there is nothing as interesting to look at as a heap of newly cut logs, the delicate colouring of their veined insides telling their life story, while they wait to bring warmth and comfort.

And so, a bit like the squirrel, we gathered in our stores for the winter, and if the snow came heavy and we were cut off from the outside world, we were safe and self-sufficient. Our wheat, which had been ground into flour at the mill, was now stored in bins to make white or brown bread. The timber barrel was full of meat and eggs came from the hens daily. When God's light faded we had the candles in the sconces and the lamp casting a soft glow around the kitchen. Facing into winter the entire work of the farm wound down, and we looked forward to the long, leisurely nights around the fire.

One of the last jobs to be done on the land was the

winter ploughing. Our work was carried out in groups but my father spent long days alone with his horses when ploughing. One winter's evening I went up in the early dusk to the field where my father was ploughing; I walked in the gap and there across the furrows of brown earth the man, the plough and his horses were silhouetted against the darkening sky. The last rays of the winter sun haloed these three in a fusion of soft light: I held my breath, afraid to intrude because I felt that I had come on a holy communion of nature, God and man. My father, who worked with the earth, had a closeness to nature and a full acceptance of its laws and the laws of God. Years afterwards, when he was a very old man, visiting him I would ask, "How are you?" and he would smile serenely and say, "Waiting". Death was as natural to him as the seasons and he had come to terms with his God out in the fields. He was not a praying man but he was a thinking man and he had thought it all out right to the end. In old age he found an inner peace; it was as if, coming near the end of the road, he looked back and saw that all the turnings had led him in the one direction.

Give Me My Shirt

HE WAS NOT blessed with a sunny disposition but possessed a razor-sharp brain and a biting wit. His role in life could best be described as a part-time travelling farmworker. How much he travelled and for how long he worked was entirely of Dan's own choosing; he was a free spirit and marched to the sound of his own drum. Trade unions would have been completely unnecessary to Dan because if conditions did not suit him he just moved on. He was master of his own destiny, but he never wronged anybody and he was completely honest.

Dan came to our house a couple of times a year and the length of his stay depended on many factors. His wardrobe consisted of a brown paper bag containing his spare shirt which he entrusted to my mother on arrival and demanded back when he made his sometimes hasty exit. Some people believe in making an entrance, but Dan was one for making an exit and his parting shot was always: "Give me my shirt – I'm going".

He usually arrived at Christmas time, because then he had the farmyard more or less to himself. At that time farmworkers went home on Christmas Eve and did not return until the 1st of February, which was the beginning of the working year, and Dan would survive longer if he had only my father to contend with, though even he was too much at times. At the end of our house was a large room where my brother slept, with a bay window opening onto the garden. There was always a spare bed in the room and some mornings Dan would be in the bed, having arrived during the night without disturbing anyone. More mornings the bed would have been slept in but Dan missing as he would have gone to bring in the cows for the early milking. He was a light sleeper and an early riser, and when he had the cows brought in he'd rattle around the kitchen and make such an infernal racket that he would wake the whole household. If anyone complained the only satisfaction Dan gave them was to remark: "Don't be sleeping your life away".

Among the other farm houses that he favoured with his presence was a widow woman who lived across the river from us. She was very mean where food was concerned and Dan enjoyed dragging the last bite from her. One day for dinner she gave him a huge plate of cabbage, which was plentiful on the farm, and a tiny bit of beef. Dan demanded more beef and got a little, with still more cabbage, and when he demanded more beef again she said:

"Dan, that heifer will be bellowing inside in you if you eat more beef."

"Jakus me, ma'am," Dan snorted, "If she will it won't be because she's looking for cabbage."

Eventually he got fed up with the widow woman and one morning, bright and early, demanded his shirt and was gone. She met him a couple of months later in town, and complained bitterly about how wrong it had been of him to desert her when she had needed him so badly.

Dan drew himself up to his full five foot two and, glaring at her from under his bushy eyebrows, he snapped: "Madam, I deserted the King of England, so where does that leave you?"

Dan usually got on well with my father, but they

could have their differences too. One winter's day Dan left the cows a bit short on hay so my father asked him to give them a little more. (The cows were kept in for the winter and tied up in their stalls in a comfortable cowhouse where they were fed with hay daily.) The next day my father went to the cowhouse to find the cows up to their ears in hay: Dan had decided to go overboard on it. My father pointed out that this was too much, whereupon Dan said:

"Jakus me, Boss, hot or cold won't please you. Give me my shirt and I'm going".

We never knew where he went to and we were never surprised when he reappeared. Once when he returned after an absence of about twelve months my father remarked that we had not seen him for a long time.

Dan looked up at him and said, "I was a guest of His Majesty the King".

We children often came under fire from Dan's erratic temper. One day during one of these forays I called him "Daneen" in a fit of annoyance. My mother intervened, reprimanding me for being so cheeky, but Dan soon put things in perspective. "Missus," he said, "children have only what they hear." We heard a rare deal of things from Dan. Across the valley from us was a large fat man with an enormous pot-belly. Dan described him one day: "Jakus me, Boss, if he was cleaned out he'd make a fine duck house". Ever after when I saw a pot-bellied man I had visions of rows of ducks sitting comfortably behind the straining waistcoat.

Dan was a little man and he carried a large walking stick with a big knob on top. He would put his two hands on top of the knob and rest his chin on them. Then with a faraway look in his eyes he would say,

"For man to man
Is so unjust,
We do not know

What man to trust.
We trusted many
To my sorrow,
So pay today
And we'll trust tomorrow."

He was a man of little sentiment and held few illusions about his fellow human beings. One day he stood watching Mick trying to put a handle on a hammer and failing to make it firm. Finally Dan could take it no longer and grabbed hammer and handle saying in a withering tone of voice: "No wonder Oisín came off the horse". When Mick's father died later in the year, leaving a lot of money after him, Dan's only comment was, "Jakus me, but he killed awful well". Death, to Dan, was nothing to mourn about, and the practicalities of life had always to be faced.

He had spent many years in the British Army and had served in the Boer War where his job had been burying the dead. He claimed that no man was ever killed whom he could not lift by himself: he was able to shift bags of coal and meal effortlessly as a result of the muscles he developed lifting dead Englishmen. A bag of coal, Dan declared, was a tidy bundle compared to a gangling corpse. After the excitement of the war Dan, with his appetite for the unusual, found the army boring so he deserted. On the night of his return to his home village he met up with his old buddies and got uproariously drunk. After closing time he staggered up the centre of the village singing at the top of his voice. At the end of the street was the barracks where a six-foot sergeant stood at the door and viewed this miniature troublemaker but Dan, oblivious to all but his own happy state, never saw the sergeant until he got a crack of the baton on top of the head. Dan's head, however, was immune to all kinds of bangs so he just stepped back and beheld his long-legged opponent. Perhaps Dan thought he was back in battle and that this was an upright corpse to shift; anyway, he put his head down and charged. He rammed the sergeant with his cast-iron skull, keeled him over his head and, grasping a long leg over each shoulder, gave the big man an upside-down piggy-back down through the village before throwing him, stunned, over the graveyard wall. He then beat a hasty retreat across the fields.

Needless to mention this encounter did not endear him to the law, who were also after him for desertion from the army. Dan enjoyed the chase and if he passed a barracks late at night he loved to leave a note on the door to annoy the occupants: "The great Dan passed this way". But finally he was caught, court-martialled and sent to jail.

The policeman who had been taken for the piggy-back informed the army sergeant who took Dan into custody that Dan had broken his mother's heart. This piece of information confirmed the sergeant's already low opinion of Dan, and when he marched the reluctant soldier around the barrack square he shouted: "Man, you broke your mother's heart: but you won't break mine!"

But neither could he break Dan because Dan thrived on controversy and *cleampar*. Finally, the army gave up on him and, after putting him on bread and water for a month, discharged him. But as Dan loved a good fight, especially with someone in uniform, he was often a guest of the prison service and of His Majesty.

When Dan ended up in court it was usually on a charge of disturbing the peace. On one occasion an attorney by the name of Burke prosecuted for the state and took great pleasure in listing out Dan's long litany of misdemeanours. Burke had a dark scar on his cheek as a result of a brawl in his student days. He completed Dan's history of wrong-doings saying, "Your Honour, this man has spent his life going from fight to fight".

"But," Dan shouted across the court, "at least I brought a clean face out of all of them!"

The entire court was highly amused, including the judge who had often suffered the long-winded, pompous Burke. The case was dismissed.

Dan had one special fighting partner whom he called "The Boar". This man was the local undertaker and as soon as Dan and himself sighted each other the coats were taken off, sleeves rolled up and a fight ensued until one or the other was knocked senseless. Dan always insisted that "The Boar" was the only man he knew worth fighting with: he provided a real challenge. Why he called him "The Boar" was known to Dan alone. One day, when they were both old men, Dan called on his opponent and just as "The Boar" stood back ready for action Dan held out his hand in friendship, saying: "We had many great fights and you gave me much enjoyment, but now I'm giving you the last round. I am going to die soon and nobody else would enjoy burying me as much as you would." Before the surprised undertaker could open his mouth Dan slapped an envelope of notes on the table and, going out the door, he looked over his shoulder and said: "I will call you Boar no more".

When Dan died he left a will bequeathing thousands of pounds to all the people he disliked most, and they were many. The fact that he did not have a penny to his name proved that Dan marched to his grave to the sound of his own drum.

A One-Way Ticket

CHILDREN WHO DIE very young leave a warm memory in the hearts of those who loved them. It is as if their candle of life, because it glows for such a short time, shines especially bright. Connie was the youngest of our family, born in the autumn of my parents' childbearing years. He was a long-legged, fine-boned little boy with silken blond hair that touched his shoulders. His birth brought great joy – if nothing else, after five daughters, he was a welcome change. An imaginative, sensitive child, he blossomed in the adoring love of this predominantly female household. My older brother at this time had left the free world of childhood behind and was finding his feet in the quicksands of adolescence.

There was just a year between Connie and me, so we grew together in early childhood like a pair of twin lambs. In my earliest memory I am sitting on a warm flagstone outside our house while Connie sits in his pram under a huge palm tree. The palm tree dominated our garden and its branches brushed against the window panes, filling the rooms at that end of the house with moving shadows.

Connie and I spent our days in the grove behind the house. The others were gone to school so we were left to our own devices. We played imaginary games beneath the trees where the ground was soft with the fallen leaves and pine needles of many years. One old tree had a huge hole in its trunk and into this we sat and pretended that we were travelling to many strange places. Because we could not see the top of this tree, as it seemed to go up and up and up, we believed that it grew into heaven. Heaven in those days was very real. The sky was our roof and the ground floor of heaven; up there were God and the angels and our cat that had died the year before. Everything that left our world finished up in heaven and we never questioned that it was a one-way ticket; after all, if heaven was where we all hoped to end up who would think of coming back?

We fed the ducks and the chickens every day and the baby calves were our favourites, though all the young animals around the yard were very much loved by us. We often visited Bill at the top of the hill, where he told us stories and gave us rides on the donkey. We could ramble through the fields and be missing for hours and nobody had need to worry because the countryside was free and safe. The only disappearance that ever created panic happened one wet winter's morning when Connie went missing. The stream at the bottom of the garden had turned into an angry torrent of flood water that backed up the garden and overflowed into the grove behind the house. Connie was nowhere to be found, and the terror was that he had fallen into the flood water. A thorough search proved that this was unlikely but the possibility could not yet be overruled. Every corner of the house and farmyard was searched to no avail. Most of this consternation sailed over my head, and I decided that I would visit our sheepdog in the haybarn who the previous week had had a litter of cuddly puppies. And there, curled up with the new mother, was Connie, sound asleep, almost indistinguishable from the pups who were draped all over him.

At night we slept together in a big bed that had a

high old-fashioned timber base and headboard. The fluffy tick filled with soft duck and goose down collected over the years from the Christmas pluckings provided warmth, and fun too as we stood on the timber head-board and dived into its comforting fullness. It had sunken pathways and fairy tunnels and countless hidden possibilities. Going to bed early, when sleep was the least of our interests, we turned the bed into a play-ground peopled by who- and whatever took our fancy; we scratched pictures on the headboard and Lowry men and women pranced around our pillows. Nobody cautioned about damaging the paintwork. There were no dolls and teddies to cuddle in bed as these were the war years and such luxuries were non-existent – but never missed. Instead, our resourceful mother provided us with two little statues, one of Saint Theresa and the other Baby Jesus. There was no shortage of statues in Irish homes at that time so every night we took our battered and chipped and much-loved statues to bed.

Once a week my mother left home to visit my grand-mother who lived a few miles down the road. She was never missing for very long but home lost some of its warmth when she was gone, and if she was not back by bedtime my oldest sister Frances did the needful. This was the case one winter's night, so my sister changed us into our night-clothes and, lighting a candle, led us upstairs to bed. The older children were trusted with candles in their bedrooms but the younger ones settled for moonlight once they were tucked up in bed.

On that particular night, however, the moon did not oblige so we were in complete darkness. Tucked up snugly in our comfortable feather tick we did not mind, but just as we were dozing off to sleep I realised that we had no statues to keep us company. We knocked on the wooden floor to summon help from the lower regions and when Frances came in answer to our call we explained about our statues. She went in search of them. After a long time she came back and tucked the statues under the bedclothes beside us.

I ran my finger over Baby Jesus and thought that he was a strange shape. Then Connie's sleepy voice whispered to me in the darkness, "Saint Theresa has a very long neck tonight". However, we were too tired to investigate any further and drifted off to sleep. We awoke the next morning to discover that instead of our two statues, which had gone missing, we were holding on to two bottles of porter.

I got my first doll the following Christmas, and Connie got a little cloth man he called Patsy. That morning I awoke and when I moved my legs something clanked off the bottom of the bed: it was a doll with a ware face, and we named her Katie Maria. We had many hours of fun with our new friends Katie Maria and Patsy, but we did not abandon our two old pals who stood guard on our bedside table.

When summer came round again we returned to the grove and our tree house. We lived in a child's wonderland and the harsh face of reality had never frowned on us. But then, suddenly, an icy draught blew around us when Connie got very sick. He had been part of my day and night, sharing every childish secret, and now suddenly he could laugh no more. He lay still and quite like a little bird in the middle of the feather bed. I sat on the floor and played with Patsy and Katie Maria. I talked endlessly to Connie, feeling that even though he couldn't answer he would know somehow that I was there. The doctor came every day and I shrank back into the corner while he examined Connie. My mother and the doctor had long discussions and I could see the pain in my mother's face.

Then one day after the doctor had been my mother told me that Connie would have to go into hospital and that he might get better, but she was not sure. Looking into my mother's stricken face I feared that Connie would never come back. Since he had got sick I had felt that something terrible was going to happen and now the certainty formed a hard lump of terror in my heart. I went up into the grove and sat into our old tree. A black car came into the yard and through the trees I watched my mother come out with Connie in her arms. He was wrapped up in a white blanket but my mother's face was whiter still.

I stayed in the tree house all day, feeling close to Connie there. Tears never came to my eyes – crying was something you did when you cut your finger. This was beyond all tears. Finally, as dusk came, I heard the pine needles crunching as someone approached. It was Bill. He sat outside the tree as he could not fit inside; just sat saying nothing while the tears ran down his face. I crept out of the tree and on to his lap, putting my arms around his neck. And so we sat, Bill and I, locked together in our terrible grief, I silently while my dear friend shuddered with great heart-broken sobs.

The next day Connie died. I did not feel any worse because it was as if it had already happened. I actually felt better because I decided that now he had left the hospital and gone to heaven he would come back. Every day I checked the tree house a couple of times in case he would be there. When this did not work out I decided it was back to the bedroom he would come. Our little room had been stripped bare and the curtains drawn, and a sulphur candle stood guttering and spluttering on our bedside table. The nuns in the hospital had given my mother a relic of Saint Theresa and a waxen pink rose which were also on the table. I hated that pink rose. In some way I had come to the conclusion that God had taken Connie and sent back this stupid rose. One day when I peeped in to see if Connie was there I could stand it no longer so I caught the rose and tore it up, petal by petal.

My refusal to accept the fact that Connie was gone must have added greatly to my mother's anguish at that time. One day in order to try to solve the problem she asked me if I would like to visit his grave. I was delighted and tore upstairs for Patsy and a bag of Connie's favourite sweets that I kept hidden under our bed: it took a long time to realize that heaven was, indeed, a one-way ticket.

Years afterwards I opened the door of a room in a strange house and the smell of a sulphur candle hit me with such an impact that a memory box in my subconscious snapped open and I was once again back in that little room. I stood rooted to the floor as tears streamed down my face while some of the anguish of those days washed over me.

Healing Place

The frosty, feathery grass
Crunched beneath my feet
As my warm valley
Caressed me in welcome;
Bejewelled with frost
The trees and grass
Sparkled in the morning sun
And across the river
The mothering mountains
Shrouded in a misty light
Stood ground. Not a sound
But the gurgling of the river
And the companions of the solitary
My feathered friends
Echoing my thoughts
Pour forth their ecstasy
In unrestrained delight.

Oh, to hold these thoughts
And this place forever
In my mind
This beloved place
So much part of me.

I stood
And let the essence
Of this balm of my growing
Soak into the inmost regions
Of my soul,
To be printed
On the back pages
Of my mind,
To be re-read

In some far distant hour
When my need
Would be great
And I could no longer
Come to this
My healing place

A Touch Of Oliver

MY GRANDMOTHER WAS a formidable old lady. She was six feet tall and, dressed in flowing black with a crochet shawl around her shoulders, she carried herself with grace and dignity. In later years she used a walking stick, but she walked with regal bearing until the day she died at ninety-eight years of age. It could be that she needed the stick to maintain law and order when she was unable to move as fast as she wanted, for while grandmothers are supposed to be loving and soft-bosomed, mine certainly did not fit into that picture: she was strong willed and domineering and ruled the house with a rod of iron. Her husband was dead with years so she ran the large farm herself and thrived on it. She was a forerunner of the struggle for equality and she was confident that most women could run a business as well if not better than men. She did just that, but in her time she was no ordinary woman. She killed her own pig and seldom sent for a vet as she could dose cattle and repair fractures like an expert. Some of her mother's people were doctors so she maintained that medicine was in her blood and, indeed, when one of her workmen was gored by a bull her fast, skilful action saved his life.

Though in some ways she was ahead of her time, in others she belonged to the era of the French Revolution. When our revolution came and the Black and Tans rampaged around the country my grandmother, a staunch Republican, was in the thick of it. Anyone on the run knew that they could get safe harbouring in her house. The Black and Tans knew this as well and many nights when the family were fast asleep the lorries drove into the yard, loud banging started on the door and the house was searched.

One night a young man called Larry, who was on the run, was asleep upstairs in the same room as her young son. Her two daughters were in another room. Suddenly the loud knocking started and she woke up. Realizing that they had not heard the warning noise of the lorries, she got out of bed slowly, hoping to give Larry time to get away, but she did not know that the house was surrounded. She still delayed in answering and the knocking turned to banging, demanding that she: "Open in the name of the King!" Eventually she opened the door and the soldiers trooped in past her. They searched the house thoroughly, even turning the bedclothes out on the floor, but finding nothing they became very annoyed because they seemed certain that there should have been somebody there.

My grandmother was a tough woman who did not know the meaning of fear: she asked them to leave now that they had searched her house. She refused to get drawn into an argument with them but stayed tight-lipped – which could not have been easy for her as silence was not one of her virtues.

The officer in charge, who had called many times, looked at my grandmother and remarked, "You remind me of my mother".

"Well, indeed," she snapped back, "your mother must not be up to much to raise a blackguard like you."

At last they left, warning her that they'd be calling again and that she'd be caught eventually. She went to the door and listened to hear the lorries starting up down the lane; then she put her children back to bed and sat by the fire for a long time. Opening the front door she checked in the half light of the dawn to make sure there was nobody about. It had happened before that the Tans had doubled back, hoping to catch them unprepared. Eventually, when she was convinced that they were safe, she stood in the middle of the kitchen and called aloud: "In the name of God where are you?"

Beside the fire in the kitchen was an old settle bed which appeared to be a timber seat when it was closed up. The Tans had checked it but when the cover did not rise they had assumed that it was just a seat. Out of this, with his face white as a sheet, rolled Larry. It had been a narrow escape. She was convinced that the Tans had known that somebody was there that night so they must have been tipped off; she suspected a family further back the valley and she never forgave them. If ever their name came up in conversation her face would darken and she would say, "Bad blood there".

When I was young I never stayed at her house as I was half afraid of her though, gradually, as she got older, she grew a little bit more mellow, or else I got braver with the years. Working for her in the house was a saintly girl called Mary who often stood between me and my grandmother's wrath. Once my grandmother had boiled a chicken and she loved the chicken broth which she had cooling in a jug on a table at the bottom of the kitchen. I decided to do a big clean up and finding this jug full of water – as I thought – I threw it out the door. When she discovered what I had done I had to spend the rest of the day out on the farm with my uncle.

As my grandmother grew older she spent more time sitting on a chair beside the fire, from where she talked non-stop. Later I regretted that I had not paid more attention to her as she had a tremendous memory and a great mind with crystal clear thinking to the very end. She was a constant reader of the *Irish Press* which my uncle brought to her every day when he went to the creamery. When he came in the door she would say: "Give me that paper until I see what old Brookeborough is saying today". All her life she took a keen interest in politics and was a fanatical supporter of de Valera. As my father was on the other side of the coin she was always slightly suspicious of him; however, politics apart, they had great respect for one another.

My grandmother had one strange chink in her armour: every couple of years she took to her bed and decided she was going to die. Admittedly this idiosyncrasy did not begin until she was over seventy so on the law of averages she could have been right. But she was no average woman and when the local doctor came he always annoyed her intensely by telling her that she was fine and had years to live. She got over this problem by contacting one of her own relations who was a doctor in the next parish. He understood what was expected of him and prescribed tablets and told her that, yes, she was quite ill and should stay in bed. My uncle regarded all this with great amusement and referred to these outbreaks as "a touch of Oliver". Why he called it this I do not know, but when he came to our house and said that "herself has a touch of Oliver" we all knew what he meant. But perhaps the doctor understood more than he got credit for. This strong woman who never showed any softness needed to go to bed and be comforted occasionally, and after a few days she would be back on her feet again.

When she had come to live on the home farm after getting married her mother-in-law, father-in-law and a brother of her husband's were already in the house before her. The brother-in-law later got married and had two children before leaving to set up in business.

Despite this extended family living together under one roof complete harmony prevailed, and all attributed this fact to my grandmother. She was a woman of many parts. She had a constant flow of visitors, including one old friend who always brought her a present of a bottle of whiskey which he drank before he went home.

She was very lucky in the fact that when my uncle married she got a splendid daughter-in-law. I was there the first morning she took over the kitchen and I was open-mouthed in astonishment at her efficiency. Grandmother had great admiration for capable people, so if the daughter-in-law had been lacking in ability it could have caused a problem. My uncle was a happy, big-hearted man who lived very comfortably between his two remarkable women. He was a sociable person who visited us regularly and always loved to have us call when we were home on holidays. In later years when television came and he had acquired a set, he put it in a cupboard. When the television was on naturally the cupboard was opened, but as soon as anybody came in visiting he turned it off and shut the cupboard. He maintained that television should be kept in its place and never take precedence over people.

When grandmother died it might have been expected that some of her old pictures might be taken down off the walls. However, when I called some years afterwards I was surprised and delighted to see the same old great-grandaunts and uncles still smiling down at me. Her daughter-in-law remembered the old lady with love and affection.

As my grandmother was such an overwhelming personality there was a danger that she might have overshadowed her only son but this, however, was not the case because, while she was forthright and domineering, he sailed through life on a sunshine cloud. They were two very different types of people. My uncle believed that life was for playing hard and working hard, and he never did anything by half measure. Sitting at the top of the kitchen table he would bang it with his fist and sing "I'm sailing along in a trolley. I feel like a big millionaire". And indeed he was very generous; when we stayed with my grandmother he never came from town without something in his pockets for us.

He put me on a pony for my first time, gave the pony a slap on the rump and set her galloping across the field with me clinging on for dear life. Finally, all the tackling which was on the pony – she had just come from the creamery – slid off and I came with it. I kicked him hard on the shins in retaliation, but he only laughed and said "Get back up now again". In a temper I did just that, but became so thrilled by this new experience that I rode the pony bare-backed all day and could not sit down for a week afterwards.

One winter we had very heavy snow which stayed on the ground for almost two months. There were drifts over six feet high along the fields and, as if this was not bad enough, a very severe flu came at the same time. When some of our family caught it we found it difficult to try to keep the cattle fed, but my uncle arrived on horse-back every day and stayed until all the work was done, even though he had to go home then and see to his own animals as well. He had a great sense of family loyalty and togetherness. "That's all that counts at the end of the day," he told me once.

On the morning of his wedding we were walking down the passage from the house on the way to the church. Suddenly, he shot in a gap and fled across the field. When I caught up with him I asked what all that was about.

"Very unlucky, Alice, to meet a foxy woman the morning you're getting married and Kate was coming around the next corner."

Kate was a red-haired woman of the roads whom we met every day, but my uncle was taking no chances this morning.

The only time I ever saw him sad was the day that Connie was buried. He sat in our kitchen, pale faced and silent, one of the images that impressed on my child's mind that this was a terrible day. I suppose that small children, to whom death is incomprehensible, can only judge its seriousness by the reaction of familiar adults. I decided that anything that could wipe the smile off my uncle's face must be disastrous.

In his autumn years my uncle developed terminal cancer. I visited him in hospital after his operation and was shattered by what illness can do to a great-hearted man. His wife nursed him in his last months and it was awe-inspiring to see the dedication and care which true love can create.

Walk The Fields

When I go home
I walk the fields,
The quiet fields
Where the warm dew
Had squelched between
My childish toes.
To sit beneath
The cool oak and ash
That sheltered
My adolescent dreams.
These trees stand
With leafy arms
Outstretched
Like lovers',
Not in passion
But with gentle
Sighs of contentment.
I watch the cows
Graze peaceful
Beside the river
Curving its way
Through furzed inches
Into the woods beyond.

This is a holy place
Where men have worked
Close to God's earth
Under the quiet heavens.

A Country Child's Christmas

CHRISTMAS IN OUR house was always magical and for weeks beforehand my toes would tingle at the thought of it. The first inkling of its reality was Santa's picture in the *Cork Examiner*: we pored over him, loving every wrinkle in his benevolent face. At first his was a small face peeping from an obscure corner, but as Christmas drew nearer his presence became more reassuringly felt as he filled a larger space on the page.

The first step in the preparations in our home was the plucking of the geese, not only for our own family but also for all our relations. A night in early December was set aside for killing and plucking; homework had to be completed quickly after school that day and when the cows had been milked and supper finished the kitchen was cleared for the undertaking. I never witnessed the actual killing because my mother performed this ritual away from the eyes of us children, but when she brought the geese still slightly flapping and warm into the kitchen I always felt that she, who was gentle by nature, had been through some sacrificial fire which but for necessity she would have avoided.

Each member of the family with arms strong enough sat on a *súgán* chair with a warm goose across their knee. My father, however, washed his hands of all this crazy carry-on and, after imparting a lecture about rela-

146

tions providing their own Christmas dinner, he set out across the fields roving to a neighbour's house where "sanity" prevailed. Strong feathers were eased off first and put into a big box and then the pure down was stowed in a smaller one. As the night wore on our arms ached and our noses itched with downy fluff, but my mother coaxed and cajoled until half a dozen geese lay starkers on the floor. With our mission accomplished we viewed each other with great merriment, our white downy heads and eyebrows lending us the appearance of white-haired gnomes. We tidied everything up then and gathered with cups of cocoa around the open fire, where my father would join us with perfect timing, bringing with him the tang of night air and frost glittering on his high boots.

During the weeks that followed the outside walls of the farmyard were whitewashed or cement washed and all the yards and passageways were brushed. Inside the house itself was washed and polished, but first the wide chimney was brushed. Standing close to our fire and peering up the chimney you could see the sky: it was a perfect Santa chimney. The kitchen floor was scrubbed, as were two tables and the chairs used to seat the lot of us. Our household seldom numbered less than ten: my parents, six of us children, a man who helped my father, a girl who helped my mother, and invariably one or two others, either miscellaneous relations or extra helpers.

The next step was "the bringing of the Christmas", as we called it. My father and mother would set out early one morning for the nearest town to buy everything that was needed for Christmas. At this stage we usually had our holidays from school and we waited expectantly all day for the homecoming; usually night had fallen by the time we heard the pony's hooves in the yard. Bubbling with excitement we watched the succession of interesting boxes being carried in and stored away in the parlour and glimpsed bottles of lemonade sparkling amidst red and white Christmas candles which foretold their own story. Other goodies were skilfully obscured from our prying fingers and inquisitive eyes.

At last, Christmas Eve dawned. We brought in the holly which we had collected from the wood the previous Sunday and in a short time holly branches were growing from behind every picture – everywhere but around the clock, which was my father's sanctum and could not be touched. Then the Christmas tree. Our house was surrounded by trees: my father planted them all his life and he loved every one of them. At Christmas he suffered deciding which of his little ones had to be sacrificed. We usually ended up with a lop-sided branch instead of a full tree, but when it was dancing with Christmas cards and balloons it always seemed a beauty. We ran streamers across the kitchen and did everything our way while my mother made the stuffing and ignored the bedlam.

A big turnip was cleaned and a hole bored in it for the candle; this was decorated with red berried holly and placed in the window. That night no blinds would be drawn so that the light would shine out to light the way for Joseph and Mary. Before supper the Christmas log was brought in and placed behind the fire in the open hearth. Banked around with sods of turf it soon sent out a glow of warmth to make the toast that was part of our Christmas supper tradition. But before anything could be eaten the Christmas candle had to be lit. We all gathered round and my father lit the candle and my mother sprinkled us with holy water. Then we sat around the kitchen table, my father at the top with my mother on his right and each of us in our own place. I feasted my eyes on the white iced cake, the seed loaf and barm brack, but most of all I gazed at the mountain of golden toast streaming with yellow butter. After supper we had lemonade and biscuits and the ecstasy of the gassy lemonade bubbling down my nose remains a memory that is Christmas for me.

Our gramophone was normally kept safe in the parlour but at Christmas it took its chance in the kitchen. Every Christmas my father bought new records and we played them non-stop. Silence was restored for the news on the radio but we young ones had no interest in the news; to us there was no world outside our own. After the news we all got on our knees for the rosary, something I never enjoyed usually, but on Christmas night it became real: this was the actual birthday of the baby. Looking out of the window into the dark night, thinking that the same stars had shone on him so many years before, in my imagination I saw the cave and the animals in the warm straw and heard the angels singing. On that far-off Christmas night I was there in my child's mind.

Off our knees my father performed the usual ritual of winding the clock. Then, standing at the foot of the stairs, his last words to my mother were: "Len, come to bed before morning". My mother, a night person who always got a second wind facing midnight, had jelly to make, stockings to darn, underwear to air around the fire. We hung our stockings on the old-fashioned crane convenient for Santa as he came down the chimney, and then mother ushered us all off to bed, the more responsible ones with a sconce and candle.

Ours was a large room with two beds and an iron cot with shiny brass railings and knobs. If the night was very cold we had a fire which cast mystic shadows along the low timber ceiling while the moon shone fingers of light across the floor. Anything seemed possible. Try as I might to keep my eyes open to see Santa appear out of the shadows, I was soon carried into the world of nod and awoke to the excruciating pleasure of sensing that Santa had been. No sensation in later life could compare with the boundless joy of those early Christmas mornings when Santa was an unquestioned reality. The gifts in the stockings were always simple and indeed often of a very practical nature but the mystique of the whole occasion gave them an added glow.

Having woken mother and father to display for them Santa's benevolence, those of us going to first Mass set out in the early dawn to walk the three miles to the church. Candles glowed from the farmhouses in the surrounding valley, making this morning very different. The lighted church welcomed us, but it was the crib rather than the Mass that was special to me, to whom these were no plaster dummies; they were the real thing. Afterwards we either walked home or got a lift from a neighbouring horse and trap. Breakfast was always of baked ham, after which the remainder of the family went into the second Mass of the day. Before leaving for Mass my mother placed the stuffed goose in a bastable over the fire with layers of hot coals on the cover. There it slowly roasted, filling the kitchen with a mouth-watering aroma.

The clattering of the pony's hooves heralded the family's arrival home and finally after much ado we were all seated around the table for the Christmas dinner. Was anything ever again to taste as good? My mother's potato stuffing was in a class of its own. We finished our dinner as the King's speech began on the radio. My father had Protestant roots and always instilled in us an appreciation of things British as well as Irish. My mother listened to the Pope, my father to the King of England, and to us they were both as much a part of Christmas as Santa. Our new records were played again and again, and toys were savoured to the full until after supper exhaustion finally won the day and we dragged our small, weary feet upstairs to bed.

It was all over for another year, but each year was another page in the book of childhood.

Show Us The Moon
Lar Redmond

Show Us The Moon offers a rich portrait of the essential Dublin and of the wit and vitality of Dublin people.

Lar Redmond, author of *Emerald Square*, writes and speaks with the authentic voice of the Liberties of Dublin where he grew up in the 1920s and 30s. His colourful, vibrant stories convey the humour and resilience of Dubliners in the face of poverty and hardship.

Of his previous book reviewers have written:
'There is a teeming sense of life and activity, and Mr Redmond is no slouch at telling a good tale well.' *Sunday Press*.
'A great read, honest and well written. . . So, dear readers, into the bin with the epic sagas. . . for this book is ideal.' *Evening Herald*.

The Heart of the City
Ronan Sheehan & Brendan Walsh

The heart of any city is its people, and in this unique book readers will encounter the people of the so-called 'inner city', people who belong to the oldest working class communities in the country.

This is no evocation of 'the rare oul' times', nor is it a study of architectural or literary heritage; neither is it a sociological study of a 'problem area'. Instead it is a portrait in words and pictures of the lives of the people who have most of all had to live with the consequences of the destruction of Dublin.

Man of The Triple Name
John B. Keane

'There is a wild animal after descending from the mountains and it is the man of the triple name, Dan Paddy Andy.'

With these words and many more Archdeacon Browne denounced the last of the great Irish matchmakers, whose 'ballrooms of romance' offered relief from grinding poverty and suffocating religiosity. Dan Paddy Andy's character and times, his wit and escapades, are magnificently described by John B. Keane.

'Hugely enjoyable.' *In Dublin.*

'Anybody who enjoys old-style storytelling at its best should reach for *Man of the Triple Name.*' *Irish Post.*

'Hilarious social history.' *Boston Irish News.*

'This lyrical, most human and highly humorous book.' *The Irish Times.*

The Bodhrán Makers:
John B. Keane

A novel of conflict and feeling; a story of people driven to rebel.

'John B. Keane's best yarn yet.' *Belfast Telegraph.*

'The book has everything. . . John B. Keane can paint real life pictures of rural life just as Thomas Hardy captured English rural life.' *Andersonstown News.*

'An important and valuable book.' *Irish Press.*

'Told with a vigour and vivacity which keeps the attention riveted.' *The Irish Times.*

'The themes of emigration and repression and the Irish natural sense of rebellion are as relevant today as they were in the 1950s.' *Evening Press.*

No Time For Love
Hugo Meenan

A novel of guerrilla warfare from a former member of both the British Army and the IRA.

'It's the best novel of its kind that I've ever read, because it's the only one. It's written from deep inside.' Eamonn McCann, *Hot Press*.

'An exciting thriller – action packed and very imaginative.' *Socialist Worker*.

'An easy but rewarding read.' *Andersonstown News*.

'His writing is not polished but it does have a capacity for stark description and his knowledge of weaponry and guerilla tactics show evidence of his experience.' *Southern Star*.

Schnitzer O'Shea
Donall Mac Amhlaigh

'This delightful novel is a satire on poets and their adopted lifestyles, on Irish intellectuals and perhaps on English land-ladies. . . Mr Mac Amhlaigh is an excellent master of English prose.' *Daily Telegraph*.

'I enjoyed the book's joyous air of leg pulling immensely and, for anyone who wants cheering up, I would recommend it unreservedly.' *Sunday Press*.

'A great read, packed with wit.' *Cork Examiner*.

'Highly amusing and absorbing.' *Irish Independent*.

'A chuckle per page.' *Irish Post*.

'It's that rare thing: an excellent comic novel.' *Evening Herald*.